About t͏͏͏͏r

Pr͏
Pre͏
in B͏
is the ͏ of the
West ͏ ͏ntral Mission and
himself became a Baptist minister
after Oxford in the 1930s.

He went on to be Professor of
Religion at McMaster University in
Canada. At Selly Oak he was very
involved in ecumenical conferences
which laid the foundation for
Churches Together. In retirement
he took on the chairmanship of the
Reform Club in the late 1980s.

About the Author

...ofessor Paul Rowntree Clifford,
...esident of the Selly Oak Colleges
...t Birmingham from 1965 to 1979
...s the son of the founders of the
...Westham Central Mission and...

EXPANDING HORIZONS

Fulfilment in later life

Paul Rowntree Clifford

A LION BOOK

Published by
Lion Publishing plc
Sandy Lane West, Oxford, England
ISBN 0 7459 3697 0
Albatross Books Pty Ltd
PO Box 320, Sutherland, NSW 2232, Australia
ISBN 0 7324 1574 8

First edition 1997
10 9 8 7 6 5 4 3 2 1 0

A catalogue record for this book is available
from the British Library

Printed and bound in Great Britain by Cox & Wyman

Contents

Chapter One

Growing Older

In this uncertain world there are two experiences from which none of us can escape: we are going to grow older and we are going to die. To say this is not morbid. It is simply stating the facts. If we are not going to take refuge in the illusions of escapism and bury our heads in the sand like the proverbial ostrich, all of us have to face what the future holds. And, whatever that may be, growing older and ultimately dying are inevitable.

Most people regard the onset of old age with foreboding; naturally so because of the prospect of physical weakness and disability, the loss of companions and friends, and the lonely adventure of death, which is the imminent and inevitable end of the road. The people and things we have loved and cherished are bound to be left behind, and the activities and achievements in which we have invested so much time and energy are destined to vanish like the castles children build in the sand at the seaside. Put like this, the prospect is bleak indeed. No wonder most people's instinctive reaction is to bury themselves in the passing moment, getting as much pleasure and satisfaction out of it as they can. If old age is progressively debilitating and death means extinction, what ground is there for hope and what alternative is there to fatalistic escapism?

This is an attitude which many people adopt in practice: momentary satisfaction with whatever life affords is all that living creatures can realistically expect. This means casting into the dustbin of history all the creative achievements of human beings in technological invention, in architecture, sculpture, music, literature and the design of beautiful things, as well as the moral grandeur of which heroes, saints and martyrs have been the outstanding exemplars. Of course, it has been argued that the achievements of the past have been built in to the heritage of the human race and that all our yesterdays have made today what it is. But that is a double-edged argument which conveniently ignores the legacy of evil that falls like a blight on the vaunted civilization of every passing age and calls into question the very idea of progress.

Even if that were not so, and a case were made out for the value of the past and the present in terms of their contribution to the future of the human race, does that future hold out any hope of value in itself for generations as yet unborn? We have to face the fact that potential disasters lie ahead, caused by the human folly of which we have seen ample evidence in the wars and ethnic and civil strife throughout this century, as well as by the unforeseen natural calamities which human ingenuity is unable to prevent. There is no likelihood, much less guarantee, that future generations will find themselves facing any different problems from ours as we have to come to terms with growing older and confront the formidable barrier of death. Rudyard Kipling's admission that 'All our pomp of yesterday is one with Nineveh and Tyre'[1] applies not only to the past and present, but to the future as well. The secularist or humanist answer to growing old and dying simply amounts to saying that the sole value in living is staying alive, and this reduces human beings to the level of the beasts of the field.

There is an alternative to this kind of fatalism, and that is what this book is all about. I am now in my eighty-third year and I have experienced what it means to grow old and infirm. As I explain to my friends, I am now living on borrowed time and do not deserve to be still alive! Death cannot be far away, but I am able to look back with gratitude on a very varied life and forward with hope to a future beyond the grave far exceeding anything I can possibly imagine. The background to this is my Christian faith and with it the conviction that life is meant to be an uphill road from the cradle to the grave and beyond. That has been my experience, which I venture to share with those of my own generation who are having to come to terms with old age and the imminence of death, but also with those who are much younger; for the way in which they anticipate the future and the storehouse of memories which they carry with them will determine the quality of life they will enjoy when they pass the age of retirement and no longer have the responsibility of earning a living.

As I look back over a long life, I find that old age has been a fulfilment of everything that has gone before, and I would not choose to go back to my youth even if I could do so. Of course, I have my regrets at many lost opportunities, mistakes and failures, but that does not alter the fact that the compensations of age far outweigh the frustrations and limitations of earlier years. From the days of my youth, I have believed that life would continue to grow more interesting as time passed and would be enriched by fresh experiences which would open doors and windows to wider horizons and deeper understanding.

This is the reverse of the common assumption that youth is the best time in one's life. When I was still a relatively young man, I used to tell high school students that no more cruel and untrue thing could be said to them than that this was the best time in their lives. If so, it would mean that they had already nearly 'had it'; that to be in your twenties was a misfortune; that to be over thirty was a disaster; and that to reach the age of forty would be firmly on a declining path to a decrepit old age! To be condemned to the emotional turmoil of the average teenager, and the boredom which often accompanies it, with no prospect of an expanding future is the lot of far too many school-leavers, aggravated by the unemployment which is all that society has to offer many of them.

In a recent article entitled 'The Blank Generation',[2] Ruth Mettens, the director of IMPACT at North London University, took the cue for her title from her son, who told her that his peers

> could be characterized by a lack of passion: the 'Don't
> Care Brigade'. Whereas earlier generations had
> assumed that they could change things, and many
> appeared to be fired with both the conviction and
> commitment to engineer such change, his own
> generation, he felt, lacks both. They are truly 'blank'.

This is a grim description of the hopeless generation for whom time has been telescoped into a vanishing present. It stores up a bleak future for those who succumb to it, and many today who find life in old age barren and dreary have sown the seeds of emptiness and discontent in their adolescence, early twenties and the rut of middle age in which they have allowed themselves to become absorbed in the transient and the trivial.

But this need not be so. Those who develop the natural curiosity and expectations of childhood throughout the following years may look forward to an expanding future which is fulfilled in the rewards of old age. Sometimes those who lapse into senility in their latter years are spoken of as having entered their second childhood. That is a complete misnomer. The greatest prize is to retain the secret of eternal childhood, and I have known many in their seventies, eighties and nineties who have been outstanding and challenging examples of this.

One of those with an enormous zest for living and an unquenchable curiosity about the future was Harris McNeill, the retired professor of New Testament Studies at McMaster University in Canada. I first met him when I joined the faculty there in 1953. Then in his seventies, he had recently been knocked down by a car and had broken his leg; nobody thought that he would ever be able to walk again. But he recovered and went on to live a vigorous life until he reached the age of a hundred. I remember following him to the library early one morning in the depth of winter, when the snow was thick on the ground. There he was, striding along, eager to find out what had recently been written in his field. He later broke his leg a second time, but again recovered, and the last picture I saw of him was taken on his hundredth birthday. He was being shown round the new medical school, curious to the very end to learn what was being done at the university.

Another striking example is found in *The Life and Letters of Hannah Whittall Smith*.[3] She was an American Quaker and author whose book *The Christian's Secrets of a Happy Life* was a best seller in the nineteenth century. This remarkable old lady was constantly shocking her prematurely aged grandchildren with her spirit of adventure, as, for instance, when she demanded that they should show her how to slide off the top of a haystack before she died! In a letter to her friends on 31 January 1903 she wrote:

I always thought I should love to grow old, and I find it more delightful than I thought. It is so delicious to be done with things and to feel no need any longer to concern myself much about earthly affairs. I seem to be on the verge of a most delightful journey to a place of unknown joys and pleasures and things here seem of so little importance compared to things there, that they have lost most of their interest for me.

I cannot describe the sort of done-with-the-world

feeling I have. It is not that I feel as if I was going to die at all, but simply that the world seems to me to be nothing but a passageway to the real life beyond; and passageways are very important places. It is of very little account what sort of things they contain or how they are furnished. One just hurries through them to get to the places beyond.

My wants seem to be gradually narrowing down, my personal wants I mean... I am tremendously content to let one activity after another go, and to await quietly and happily the opening of the door at the end of the passageway, that will let me into my real abiding place. So you may think of me as happy and contented, surrounded with unnumbered blessings, and delighted to be 71 years old.[4]

When I first read this exhilarating book, I was struck again by the dreary boredom of so many teenagers. Failure to fill the vacuum of youth with anything that offers promise for the future goes far to explain the frustrated mentality which finds expression in vandalism, hooliganism, the drug culture and the craving for excitement which now threatens the very fabric of our society.

I remember being bored when I was at school. Looking back on this, I believe it was due to unimaginative teaching, which did not stimulate my curiosity and which only began to be rectified when I had the privilege of spending six years at Oxford. But, even then, horizons were very limited and only as the years have passed have they broadened out to the point where infinity becomes an exciting challenge. I can honestly say today that I am never bored; there is always something to be explored. Entering a library cuts me down to size in the realization that there are vast numbers of books I will never have time to read and fascinating questions I will never have the opportunity of pursuing. Old age has brought with it the appreciation of how little I know and an introduction to ideas which are only beginning to be formed. Moreover, there are people whom I will never meet and adventures which I will never undertake. This is where increasing physical weakness becomes an insurmountable obstacle, but it is compensated for by the richness of memory and the knowledge that the limitations of old age only point to the possibility of wider vistas and more comprehensive human relationships.

This experience of growing older is encapsulated in some lines of Robert Browning in 'Rabbi ben Ezra':

Grow old along with me!
The best is yet to be,
The last of life, for which the first was made:
Our times are in His hand

Who saith, 'A whole I planned,
Youth shows but half; trust God: see all, nor be afraid!'

I do not believe that I have a vested interest in citing this quotation simply because I am an octogenarian; it has been my attitude and expectation from a very early age. When young couples used to come and see me about getting married, I tried to penetrate their starry-eyed and natural euphoria by saying that the honeymoon would not be the peak of their relationship from which they would gradually descend into the doldrums and a dreary old age. The reverse is what they should expect: the first year of mutual adjustment being the most difficult, followed by a process of growing together in understanding and experiencing the joys of a shared life. The failure to realize that the rewards of marriage are to be achieved only by surmounting difficulties and misunderstandings and working at the relationship over a period of years is the cause of so many breakdowns and divorces in modern society.

Many of the problems of old age, as I have said, are attributable to seeds sown in earlier years. Those whose horizons have been confined to the sensations of the passing moment, or who have later allowed themselves to get into a rut of trivialities, will have no store of experience on which to depend when they reach pensionable age. There is nobody more to be pitied than those who dread retirement and find the prospect before them bleak and empty. A full life, a growing curiosity and an enrichment of experience are the capital which yields abundant interest in old age.

There is, however, another side to the picture. Ageing has its problems as well as its rewards. Increasing physical weakness and the impairment or loss of faculties, such as sight and hearing, are handicaps that many old people have to face. The incidence of strokes and coronary attacks which, while not fatal, leave the sufferer with severe restrictions on mobility is likewise high among the over-seventies. Then there is the experience of dying, sometimes protracted and painful, which is probably the greatest fear in the minds of people as they grow older. In the light of these considerations how can it be plausibly maintained that old age and death may be anticipated with hope as the climax of life and the fulfilment of all our strivings over the years?

Here I must set out my credentials, such as they are, for venturing to answer these questions; for it is only on the basis of personal experience that anyone has the credibility to speak, however tentatively, about matters which affect people so differently and which may touch on sensitive nerves where the reader has had to watch the suffering and death of someone he or she has loved. That is my excuse for writing so much about myself. But this is not an autobiography, certainly not of the usual kind which traces a life from its origins to the present. This I attempted to do in an earlier publication.[5] Here in this book I start the other way round, looking back on what I have experienced and trying to see what its significance turns out to be in the light of the ending of the road. One of the main benefits of old age is that you are free of ambition as far as this life is concerned and so you are enabled to take a more detached view of people and events than is possible in the cut and thrust of a busy life.

I am only too aware that my experience has been different from that of others who have had to face frustrations, pain and illness far exceeding anything to which I have been subjected. Indeed, suffering may seem more destructive and inexplicable when experienced in childhood and youth than in later years. Nevertheless, I have had to come to terms with the problems of infirmity and the prospect of death, and I am conscious that illness may carry with it the onset of pain and suffering, which for a great many people is the most intractable problem of old age. Many, indeed, regard it fatalistically as the probable expectation of those approaching the end of life.

In the chapters which follow, I shall try to deal with these and other problems of old age as honestly as I can. But my starting-point is the experience of a life of expanding horizons and years of retirement, which have proved to be its most interesting and stimulating climax. So, before tackling the inevitable problems, I want to explain how the treasure house of memory and the opportunity for mature reflection have made old age, for me, such an enriching experience.

Chapter Two

The Storehouse of Memory

One of the greatest blessings of old age is the gift of memory. It stands to reason that the older we grow the more we have to remember. Of course, this has to be qualified in those cases where elderly people suffer from loss of memory, though this is the loss of the power of retrieval, not the loss of that which is capable of being recovered. What is forgotten is not necessarily lost; indeed the fact that we all remember different things at different times, and recall events after a long interval in which they have been totally absent from our minds, shows that we should be on our guard against thinking that memory is a faculty which can easily be explained. We are led astray by the use of one word to cover two quite different things: memory as *the act of remembering* and memory as *that which is remembered*.

Memory, understood objectively as that which is

remembered, is a priceless treasure house. To compare it with a computer presents us with difficulties which seem to be beyond the compass of our imagination, since this entails the belief that the whole range of our experience, including the minutest detail, is stored in the brain. Such a conclusion makes the invention of the most sophisticated computer look like child's play by comparison. Any explanation would break down which depended on an analogy with the disks we use on our word processors, from which we can erase anything we like and thus make them manageable and intelligible. But the equivalent of a disk from which nothing can be erased, yet most of which is beyond the power of recall, presents a considerable challenge to our comprehension. It might be suggested that the details of our past which we cannot remember are erased like words on a disk, but this would not account for the fact that we remember the most trivial things after a long interval in which they have been entirely absent from consciousness. If the brain is the storehouse of memories, it must be a comprehensive storehouse beyond the powers of our imagination, vastly more extensive than the content of what is actually remembered.

This may be the most plausible theory that can be devised. In any case, to take the debate further would be beyond the scope of this book. We are left with the mysterious faculty we have of selectively recalling past experiences, often quite randomly, though sometimes at the cost of considerable effort.

Difficult as it is to fathom the mystery of the process whereby we remember anything, the fact remains that we do have the power of random or deliberate recalling of the past, and this is a precious attribute of old age, even when certain memories appear to have been altogether lost. Memories may be of various kinds: many trivial, some involving places and people of particular concern to us, some affecting other people or public events of widespread interest. The older we are, the richer is the storehouse if we have filled it with that which is of enduring value. To dwell on the past is not to be dismissed as self-indulgence; it has value in itself and can stimulate fresh creativity even when physical powers have declined. The bleakness of the lives of many old people can be traced back to a preoccupation during youth and middle age with the trivial and with the satisfaction of passing sensations. We reap what we sow, and the quality of life in old age is largely determined by our past. Saving money through pensions and thrift is important for securing physical care and comfort when we are no longer able to work or be physically active. But concentration on material safeguards to the neglect of enriching the future by the quality of those experiences which contribute to a fulfilled life is a recipe for a bleak and unsatisfying old age. We become what we have grown to be, and memory is the treasure house which enshrines the past in the prospect of an expanding future.

Nevertheless, old age is a period of increasing inactivity. That is why it is dreaded by those whose lives have been invested in a constant whirl of activity, much of which in retrospect is seen to have been unimportant. Enforced retirement at a certain age offers a bleak prospect to those whose paid employment has dominated their lives at the expense of developing a wide range of interests and a circle of friends which can be enjoyed in the greater freedom that retirement affords. Even for those who look forward to this prospect, the possibility of different forms of activity such as hobbies and travelling, rewarding as these can be, may have their limits. The time may come when physical weakness frustrates the opportunities which have long been anticipated. Then the treasure house of memory can come into its own. Bustling activity which often goes round in circles is not the be all and end all of existence. Contemplation can be just as satisfying, provided we have accumulated enough experiences to provide the substance of our reflections. And when memory, in the sense of the power of recall, begins to fail, a peaceful end to life on earth can be its own reward.

Each person must speak or write from his or her own experience, and I recognize that I have been singularly fortunate, not only in my home and upbringing, but in my marriage and the fascinating things I have been enabled to do. I hope that this does not make me insensitive to those whose problems in growing old and dealing with infirmity have been much greater than mine, but rather that sharing my own experience may be of some value to others who find the prospect of growing old both daunting and even frightening. That is my excuse for venturing to recount my own personal reminiscences.

I have been privileged to enjoy a fruitful and happy retirement, to which many people beyond my immediate family circle have contributed. In my autobiography *An Ecumenical Pilgrimage*, to which I referred in the opening chapter, I spoke of three phases of retirement, the first two of which, leading from 1979 to the death of my wife, Marjory, in 1988, were full of varying and interesting responsibilities. The great advantage of relinquishing paid employment is that you can do things in your own time without any sense of pressure to conform to expectations that are imposed upon you. When Marjory died, I had to start life over again at seventy-five, and so I decided to look up old friends whom I had not seen for years. Among them was Dorothy, who had been with me on the staff of the West Ham Central Mission in London during the Second World War. She had been my first secretary, but we had lost touch for over forty years, during which she had pursued a nursing career, ending up as the Deputy Chief Nursing Officer at the Ministry of Health. We decided to share the rest of our lives together, and that began my third retirement. Some months after our marriage, my mobility began to be affected by a series of illnesses, and I am afraid Dorothy found she had taken on what our local doctor described as 'damaged goods'! My increasing disability has imposed a heavy burden on her, but I have been wonderfully cared for and this has enabled me to experience the joys of a contemplative retirement such as I have been describing. The infirmity of old age does not necessarily diminish the zest for living or the enjoyment of new experiences; it simply means that life is different, with fresh problems and opportunities.

All of us have to adapt to changing circumstances throughout our lives, but to do so becomes increasingly pressing as we grow older. Adaptability in earlier years makes this easier when our physical powers become weaker and we find that we are unable to do many things which were within our capacity in the past. That is why old age is so much more frustrating for some people than for others. In the United States some years ago a survey undertaken of a group of men and women over sixty-five years of age showed that 25 per cent were successfully creative, 34 per cent were struggling towards creativity, and in the remaining 40 per cent creativity had been virtually submerged. It is a fair inference that this was largely due to the way they had adapted to change earlier in life.

But when physical powers become progressively limited, the treasure store of memory becomes increasingly important. It largely consists of trivial things, though these spark off recollections of much greater significance. For example, one of my most vivid and recurrent memories is of the lock on the front door of Settlement House at the West Ham Central Mission, where I began my ministry over fifty years ago. It was operated by a peculiar metal button which I have never seen anywhere else. To open the door you had to hold the back of it between two fingers and then press the centre with your thumb to release the catch. Why such a knob should have lodged itself so vividly in my brain I cannot possibly say, but the memory of it starts a chain of associations with West Ham which cover the next seventeen years and include the dramatic events of the Nazi air raids on London's Dockland during the Second World War.

Memories of places form an important part of the

past which we constantly recall. I suspect that the houses in which we have lived make indelible marks upon our minds because of their association with those in our family who have meant most to us. Thomas Hood's poem[1] evokes sentiments which all of us can recognize:

I remember, I remember
The house where I was born,
The little window where the sun
Came peeping in at morn;
He never came a wink too soon
Nor brought too long a day;
But now, I often wish the night
Had borne my breath away...

I remember, I remember
The fir trees dark and high;
I used to think their slender tops
Were close against the sky:
It was a childish ignorance,
But now 'tis little joy
To know I'm farther off from Heaven
Than when I was a boy.

The pathos and wistfulness of these lines unhappily find an echo in the experience of many people. I am grateful that I can look back on twelve homes in which I have lived, all linked with happy memories: four in my childhood and youth which were occupied by my parents; one in West Ham during the early years of my marriage to Marjory; three in Canada, where I was on the faculty at McMaster University; the President's house on the campus of the Selly Oak Colleges in Birmingham; and then three in retirement: Crinan Cottage at Dalbeattie in Galloway, the bungalow in Middleton Cheney near Banbury which Marjory and I acquired to be nearer our family, and lastly Dorothy's flat overlooking the sea at Eastbourne. Homes are not simply bricks and mortar; they are made by people dear to us—in my own case, first by my mother and then by my wife. There, life finds its centre from which all activity radiates.

It is tragic when the memory of home is associated with strife and discord. I shall never forget the occasion when on a visit to Canada in 1947 I was invited to speak at the chapel service of a leading girls' school in Toronto. The headmistress said that if any of the girls wanted to speak to me after the service I would be glad to see them in an adjoining room. I never expected anyone to come, but I hardly had time to sit down when there was a tentative knock at the door and two children aged about ten or eleven came in and nervously perched themselves side by side on a sofa. When I asked what they wanted to say, one of them murmured shyly, 'It's not me; I've come with my friend'; the other then burst out: 'My mother and father are going to be divorced before I go home at the end of the term, and I don't know what to do.' Never shall I forget the anguish on the face of that child. Many parents do not seem to realize the cost to their children of their failure to relate creatively to one another, and the memories of far too many children are scarred by images of the bitterness and strife which have led to the break-up of their families.

My own memories of a stable home and family life are traced back to my father's childhood home in Sunderland, to which as small children my brother and I were taken for seaside holidays. It was dominated by my grandmother, who was the centre of a scattered family of uncles and aunts who gravitated there whenever possible and gave me my early experience of an extended family. Vivid details of these childhood visits, such as 'the Sunderland cake' and ginger-nuts, made a lasting impression, which stands out amidst the happy memories of days long past.

Houses are often associated with people who had something to do with their design. The first home of our own which Marjory and I had was a bungalow built by Arly Girard, an old-fashioned craftsman who worked by himself, designing and constructing it from start to finish without any assistance. Marjory and I had rented an apartment when I first joined the faculty of McMaster University in 1953. Having spent the early years of our marriage in the manse on the compound of the West Ham Central Mission, our intention on going to Canada was simply to take a break after the exhaustion of the war years and their aftermath. We had no thought of staying more than a year before returning to England, but the professor-designate, whose place I had been temporarily invited to fill because of his unexpected illness, proved to be terminally sick and the appointment was offered to me. Nothing else having appeared on the horizon, I accepted the offer on a year-to-year basis and we had to find somewhere to live. Arly Girard was in the process of building a small bungalow on the edge of a wooded ravine near the university, and this seemed an ideal location. We were able to watch a superb craftsman at work, who treated the materials he handled, particularly wood, with an almost religious reverence; indeed he saw the building of a house as an offering to God, and it was a great privilege to become the beneficiaries of what was probably the last example of his handiwork.

Houses, of course, are not memorable simply for their own sake. It is the people associated with them—our family, neighbours and friends—who are most prized in the storehouse of memory. Binkley

Crescent, where we now lived, was the home of people who became our very close friends. Notable among them were Herbert and Mildred Forbes. He was a highly respected insurance agent in Hamilton, the epitome of a public-spirited and cultured businessman, whose transparent integrity was recognized by all who came into contact with him. He had a long-standing interest in British history, in which he felt his Canadian citizenship was rooted, and, although he had not had an opportunity to travel beyond the American continent, he cherished the hope that one day he would visit the British Isles. His dreams were realized many years later and we were able to entertain him and his wife in Britain.

Houses are associated with treasured memories of people who never became famous, but who were the salt of the earth. When my tenure of the professorship at McMaster University was prolonged for several years, we concluded, mistakenly as it was to turn out, that the rest of our days were to be spent in Canada; and so we began to think about building a house in which we could live for the rest of our lives. We acquired a plot of ground in the nearby township of Ancaster and looked for a builder who would fulfil our requirements. That is how we came to meet Jack McNaught. Friends had told us that we should approach him and see whether he would do what we wanted, but we were warned that he had virtually retired and was only likely to take on any more work if he could be really interested in the project. His father and grandfather had built houses before him, but his only son was a candidate for ordination to the Anglican ministry and therefore there would be nobody left to carry on the family business.

When Jack came to see me, I wondered how we would get on. His dour appearance and gruff exterior did not hold out any promise of an easy relationship, but he listened to what I had in mind. Then he said, 'I'll build you that house on two conditions: the first is that you'll not let any architect come near the place; they know nothing about building houses; and the second is that once you've agreed that I should build it, you won't interfere with me until I hand over the key!' I was impressed by his confidence and told him to go ahead.

I had raised a mortgage to cover the whole cost on the strength of my professorship at McMaster, though this was to cause me some anxiety two years later, when I was unexpectedly invited to return to England to become President of the Selly Oak Colleges in Birmingham. But I was able to watch a first-rate builder erecting stage by stage the house of our dreams: spacious living and dining rooms, panelled study, fully-equipped modern kitchen with ample space for breakfast, and a basement running the length of the house for recreation purposes, opening out into the garden behind. The walls were insulated from the foundations upwards and wired throughout for plugging in a telephone anywhere. When the key was handed to me, I could not fault any detail in the design or construction. The memory of Jack McNaught's house was to set a standard of workmanship which I found sadly lacking on my return to England, but it was to serve as a pattern for all the building developments for which I was later to be responsible.

The house on the Selly Oak campus was an entirely different proposition. It had been built for my predecessor on a very tight budget, and his wife liked plenty of light; the outside walls were mainly of glass and it seemed to have been designed more for heating the garden than the rooms inside! Jack McNaught would have had apoplexy if he had seen it! Since it was in the middle of the campus, it was like living in a goldfish bowl. We were able to modify its inconvenience as time passed but, in spite of the exciting challenge presented by my new appointment and the rewards of being given the most fascinating job I could conceive, we could not help thinking wistfully of Ancaster and the house Jack had built for us there.

It was not until my retirement in 1979 that we were able to think again of a home of our own. We had acquired a little cottage a mile and a half out of Dalbeattie when on holiday in Scotland. We never intended to retire there, but to have it as a base from which we could find somewhere to live for the rest of our days. It was an old 'butt and ben', probably dating from the seventeenth century, with a loft above the two rooms to which access could be obtained by a ladder from a ramshackle extension. This had fairly recently been added in the form of the letter T, and comprised a kitchen, a bathroom and a small sitting room. We saw its potential for imaginative alterations and, our modest offer being accepted on the last day of our holiday, we managed to secure the services of a young architect in Dumfries to whom we explained what we had in mind. He promised to draw up sketch plans overnight which we could look at on our way back to Birmingham the next day. When we saw them, he had designed exactly what we wanted. As we were due to go on sabbatical leave from the Selly Oak Colleges to Central and South America, we had to leave everything in his hands, trusting that the result would match our expectations.

When we returned some months later we found the work almost finished. The ramshackle extension had been completely gutted, the stem of the letter T forming a dining hall with a parquet floor, and the living-room extended with French windows opening on to a patio facing a long garden, at the end of which was the Solway Forest. A breathtaking view of the mountains of the Lake District in the distance formed a glorious background on a fine day. A bedroom, with bathroom en suite, and a modern kitchen, utility room and additional bathroom had been added at the back without spoiling the old-world view of the 'butt and ben' from the road. We called it 'Crinan Cottage' because of its association with our first holiday together at Crinan, further to the north, with Marjory's father and mother, before we were married.

This reconstruction introduced us to Gordon, another craftsman like Arly Girard and Jack McNaught. Gordon had been virtually responsible for all the work thus far done, and we were able to watch him complete the job. When he had finished, the result was so attractive and the setting so idyllic that we were loth to look for any other property. Thus, Crinan Cottage became our home for the next five years, introducing us to a new circle of friends. Notable among these was the nearby farmer, Stanley Edmunds, and his wife. They took these city-dwellers, inexperienced in country life, under their wing and, if we faced any emergency, like the failure of the well which supplied our water, Stanley would be at our gate with his tractor. He would deliver a load of logs before Christmas and invite us to the

Scottish New Year celebrations in his farmhouse. He was one of the most versatile men I have known, finding time for expert knitting, from which our first grandchild benefited, and mending clocks and watches - of which he had a large collection in the farmhouse. His wife, Jenny, was a splendid cook and we enjoyed their hospitality at many a meal.

To be part of a rural community was an entirely new experience for both of us, and this first phase of retirement was an unexpected enrichment to the storehouse of memory. However, we had to face the fact that we were growing older and could not expect to live much longer in such an isolated spot, half a mile from the Edmunds' farmhouse on one side and the same distance from our nearest neighbour on the other. The crunch came when our daughter in the Midlands telephoned to ask whether we would be down south in a fortnight's time to babysit while she and her husband attended their best man's wedding. The thought of 250 miles of motorway between us and a family emergency, coupled with the responsibilities that necessitated frequent train journeys to London and Birmingham, made it clear that we should have to move.

So we had to forsake our first real home back in Britain and look for somewhere closer to our daughter near Stratford-on-Avon and our son in London, providing good road and rail communications for the responsibilities I had undertaken. Marjory settled on the Banbury area, where she found an attractive bungalow in the village of Middleton Cheney. Sadly, we had no sooner moved house than we discovered that she had contracted breast cancer, and her courageous battle against the spreading disease cast a shadow over the next four years. After her death in 1988, to which I have already referred and which I shall be describing in a later chapter, I began my third retirement by marrying Dorothy White and moving into her beautiful flat overlooking the sea at Eastbourne, where I am now reflecting on the blessings of old age.

My reason for reminiscing about the houses in which I have lived is that they have evoked memories of some of the people connected with them, and in recording them it is my hope that it will stimulate the reader to do likewise; for in the last resort it is people who really matter and the relationship we are privileged to have with them. Significant history is not necessarily made by the so-called 'great and good', but by ordinary men and women whose names are unknown except to a relatively small circle. According to Christian faith and tradition, however, they find their ultimate fulfilment in the eternal purpose of God.

Chapter Three

Creative Remembering

Memory in old age need not be self-indulgence, dwelling on the past and regretting that it cannot be relived. I hope I have said enough in the last chapter to show that it can open a rich storehouse of enjoyment and contemplation to which many people have contributed, and help us to achieved tranquillity when, to use words from a prayer in the Anglican Prayer Book, 'the fever of life is over and our work is done'. Memory then becomes the fulfilment of life. But it can be much more than that, as remembering brings back the past creatively.

This is the significance of the national observance of Remembrance Sunday in Great Britain, with services at the Cenotaph in London and at war memorials in every town and village. The great majority of those who take part in these ceremonies were born after the Second World War was over. But it is not for veterans of that and other conflicts alone that remembering is significant. I think of the celebrations of the fiftieth anniversary of VE Day, when the emphasis was on peace and reconciliation. That is the goal to which every energy has to be bent. Remembrance Day is not simply an occasion for recalling the past, but a spur to the creation of a world in which hostility, strife and violence will cease to prevail.

When, on these special occasions, we are enabled to remember the sacrifice of those who gave their lives in past conflicts, the older ones amongst us recall the names and faces of individual people, men and women whom we have known and loved, the value of whose lives cannot be measured in the general act of remembrance. Wartime leaders on the battlefield and in politics are memorialized in biographies, but for most of us it is Ian, Harry, Chris and Margaret of whom we think and whose memories we preserve as a spur to ourselves and others to leave this world better for having lived and died in it.

But this is not restricted to those who have fallen in battle. Many others have contributed to the richness of our personal heritage, and every reader will have a personal gallery of names and faces who in some way have shaped his or her life and whose influence for good or ill is passed on to those who come after. In reflecting on my own gallery of names, I hope it will evoke memories on the part of the reader which will serve as a reminder of the significance of every human being by whose contribution the future is conditioned.

In the last chapter I wrote about the people particularly connected with the houses in which I have lived. Now I propose to broaden the canvas to the major events in my life and the places I have visited. These conjure up a host of memories of all sorts of people, some famous, the majority unknown to any but a small circle of acquaintances and friends. However, the famous may soon pass into obscurity, while those who are relatively unnoticed may make a lasting contribution to the welfare and happiness of other people. Viewed in the light of eternity 'the last shall be first and the first last'.

One memory shades into another as I look back and try to understand how old age has been shaped by the past; but there are turning-points in everyone's life which may not have seemed so important at the time, though in retrospect they may be seen to have been decisive.

The first of these was the day I left home for boarding-school at the age of thirteen. It was my introduction to a potentially hostile world. My childhood had been spent in the protection and care of loving parents. Now I had to stand on my own feet among older boys whose main preoccupation seemed to be making 'new bugs' conscious of their inferiority and worthlessness. I was miserable and begged my father to take me away. I am profoundly glad he did not; for, whatever the defects of Mill Hill in those days as an educational institution, it provided the context in which I began to discover the meaning of responsibility.

I pondered a long time before using those precise words because to have said that I began to learn to stand on my own feet would have distorted the crucial decision which was to govern the rest of my life. I remember walking round Top Field at Mill Hill all by myself in my first term, wrestling with the question of whether I could survive the pressures to conform to a way of life which seemed to be in sharp distinction from that to which I had been accustomed at home. I decided that I could not unless I made a firm commitment to live as a Christian, accepting the Lordship of Jesus Christ and putting myself in his hands. This led me to ask my father, who was a Baptist minister, to baptize me on the following Easter Day. That was the most important and far-reaching decision I have ever made and, in spite of many doubts and perplexities over the years, it is one I have never regretted. It has given me the perspective for all later decisions and, as I look back on over eighty years of varied experience, it has provided the pattern in the light of which I can now distinguish between the wheat and the chaff.

Mill Hill introduced me to the appreciation of music, which becomes of increasing value with the passage of the years and is one of the treasures of old age. It began with membership of the school choir which rehearsed four times a week under the direction of Laurie Cane, the music master, whose infectious enthusiasm turned a voluntary activity—a rarity in the regimented curriculum—into an exercise which nobody would miss. I also remember with gratitude the gramophone recitals of classical music provided by the Spanish master in one of the classrooms on Sunday evenings, and the introduction to the Gilbert and Sullivan operas under the tuition of Mary Elliott, the wife of Victor, my housemaster, both of whom became valued friends in later years.

More important still was the beginning of a lifelong friendship with John Terry, who was learning the piano at the time. I remember hearing him practise one of the Bach Preludes and Fugues, unable to master a short passage and playing the same bars over and over again. Suddenly the penny dropped, and from that moment Bach for me became the prince of composers.

On leaving school, John was articled to the legal firm of Denton, Hall and Burgin. From there he joined the Film Finance Corporation, of which he subsequently became director, sponsoring many of the best-known British films. His reputation was such that Harold Wilson invited him to chair the government enquiry into the industry and he was knighted in the Prime Minister's Retirement Honours List. He died just a fortnight before these lines were written, and I remember him as one of the kindest men I have known as well as an entertaining companion and friend. We had explored together the joys and opportunities of retirement, and throughout our lives we had shared many memories of boys who were at school with us. Some subsequently became famous, such as Dennis Thatcher, husband of the former Prime Minister, and the well-known broadcaster Richard Dimbleby.

The second milestone in my saga of memories was my ordination to the Christian ministry in 1938 as a member of the staff of the West Ham Central Mission, which my father and mother had founded during London's notorious dock strike of 1905. My ordination almost coincided with the outbreak of the Second World War, which evokes memories of many remarkable people and their courage and tenacity in facing the onslaught of the Luftwaffe on the capital. I have told the story of the West Ham Central Mission in *An Ecumenical Pilgrimage*. Here, I simply want to recount the memory of a few people, some famous, some unknown, connected with it.

Almost the first who comes to mind is General Sir John Shea who was a frequent visitor to the manse in the Mission compound during the intense air raids on Dockland. He had formerly been Commander-in-Chief in India, but during the war he was Scout Commissioner for London. He was a striking figure, dressed in khaki uniform with rows of ribbons on his chest, swathed in a huge khaki cloak surmounted by a scout hat, wearing a monocle and carrying a long staff. His appearance caused a stir wherever he went, not least in the United Services Club! He told me that his introduction to the Scout movement was being invited, or rather dragooned, by Baden Powell to accompany him to a rally in the East End of London. He described how they made their way down a back street to a hall from which a tremendous noise was emerging. It was packed with boys, large numbers of little Wolf Cubs filling the space in front of the platform, and cheering with excitement at the sight of their famous leader. Baden Powell simply stepped forward, held up his hand, and there was dead silence. Then he looked down at the throng of Wolf Cubs and said, 'Do you know, you're the ugliest crowd I've ever seen!' They shrieked with delight, and Sir John said that from that moment he was captivated by the influence of a man who could make such an impression on a crowd of boys.

At any rate, Sir John was a great source of encouragement to us in those dark days of the Blitz. We had a large group under a remarkable scout master, Fred Beagles—a giant of a man with a magnetic personality as far as boys were concerned and who, with them, did yeoman service in manning the large shelter we administered, supporting the rescue services and sustaining morale. Sir John Shea was a regular source of encouragement to them, as he was to many others, and kept the rest of us from feeling isolated. But my chief memory of him is his unfailing old-world courtesy. Whenever he spent a night with us at the manse, a letter of thanks would follow ending with the words, 'Please do my humble duties to your mother.' I shall say something more in a later chapter about what he said to me about life after death. But here I record his memory with gratitude as representing the courtesy and consideration of a true gentleman, which is sadly lacking in the casual brashness of conventional behaviour today.

Another remarkable person who came to our aid at the height of the Blitz was Eny Strutt—The Honourable Mrs Arthur Strutt, to give her her full title, though her complete absence of snobbery makes the more familiar name seem more appropriate. She feared God, but no man, and was ruthless in her championship of the disadvantaged, using her considerable influence with those in high places to cut through red tape and right a wrong wherever she detected it. I have never met anyone with a greater passion for social justice concentrated on the misfortunes of individual people. This could lead to embarrassing situations, as when she arrived on my doorstep to tell me that she had found disgraceful conditions in one of the surface shelters in Canning Town and that she had told the Home Secretary, Ellen Wilkinson, to come down at once and see the conditions for herself. Eny told me that I must show the Home Secretary the shelters and demand that something should be done. I had to explain that a government minister could not be brought on a goose chase on the basis of the neglect of one shelter! But Eny was irrepressible. I remember her fury when we had been campaigning to get first aid equipment installed in the public shelters, and she had found a young man lounging in a chair in the shelter under the Silvertown Way with instructions to see that nobody touched the equipment that had been installed! If she spotted bureaucratic inefficiency, she hunted it down like a terrier and she was not afraid of threatening the wrath of 10 Downing Street if wrongs were not righted. Eny was like a breath of fresh air when such people were few and far between.

I continued to keep in touch with her after the

war and visit her from time to time in her beautiful home at Tetbury in Gloucestershire. The last time I saw her was just after her ninetieth birthday, which had been celebrated by members of her family taking her for a flight in a helicopter over southern England. By then she was confined to a wheelchair, completely crippled with arthritis, but still fighting battles for people she had heard had been unjustly treated.

One of my most vivid memories of the Blitz was that of an old lady who came every night to the shelter we manned in the basement of one of our buildings, and who, without a word of complaint, sat upright in a wooden chair because she could not lie down. I do not remember her name, but she typified the heroic East Enders who defied the onslaught of the Luftwaffe. I often wished one of these unknown old people could have been honoured with the George Cross as representing countless others. Of one thing I am sure: Eny Strutt would have been delighted to be associated in memory with her; for she was like one of those whom Eny was concerned to champion.

A public figure of the time who stands out in my memory is Ernest Brown, the much vilified Minister of Labour in Neville Chamberlain's pre-war cabinet, who was appointed Minister of Health when Churchill took over the reins of government. He was not everyone's favourite politician, but my memory of him is connected with two incidents which give a glimpse of his underlying character.

I was responsible for arranging a service for civil defence workers in the Memorial Church of the West Ham Central Mission and I had invited Ernest Brown, a prominent Baptist layman, to deliver the address. When the service was over I asked him whether I should summon his ministerial car. 'Car!' he exclaimed. 'I'm going back by bus. I wouldn't use my car in wartime for what wasn't official government business.'

The second incident occurred a little while later when I had been invited to participate in the ordination and induction service of one of our young men from West Ham to the ministry of the church of Westbourne Park in West London. Because of the air raids, the service was held on a Saturday afternoon. It had just begun when Ernest Brown entered the door at the back and took his seat in the congregation. After it was over, I went down the aisle to greet him and express my pleasure and surprise at seeing him there. 'Oh,' he said, 'I felt I ought to come and say my prayers for a young man beginning his ministry here in times like these.' That was what he considered to be a priority for a Saturday afternoon, when most busy people, let alone a wartime cabinet minister, would feel they were entitled to snatch an hour or two of rest. In these days, when sleaze and corruption in public life occupy the headlines in the news, I cherish the memory of someone not for his public contribution to the wartime effort, but for himself and the kind of person he was.

In Sir John Terry, Sir John Shea, Eny Strutt and Ernest Brown I have selected memories of those who were well-known in film, military, social and political circles; but my years at West Ham were enriched by many people who have all been forgotten, except by a very few, yet whose lives have had an abiding value which at least equals those whose names will be recorded in the annals of history.

My own life was influenced and my ministry supported by a great many people, among whom were the deacons of the Memorial Church, a group of men and women elected to serve as its governing council. They were a mixed company, covering a wide variety of occupations: a small business man, the secretary to the Ford Motor Works at Dagenham, a local government officer, a printer, the secretary to a publisher, a medical practitioner, a chemist, a docks superviser, a retired tram driver and a labourer at Beckton Gas Works. It would be invidious to distinguish between them and tedious for those who did not know them to attempt to describe them in any detail. I simply select one of them as representative of them all because he illustrates what an impact an ordinary man can have on other people and because his memory stands out above that of many others who would be regarded as far more important according to common standards for appraising anyone's worth.

John Keogh received nothing more than an elementary education and worked as a labourer until his retirement. He lived to be over ninety years of age, possessing the rarest of gifts—a serene inner tranquillity which was the fruit of a lifetime of devoted Christian discipleship in the service of others. No one on earth will ever reckon how much good he did; mere hints were given by stories told of visits to those in trouble, nights spent in the homes of the sick and dying, simple acts of kindness done without prompting on anyone's part. He never achieved anything spectacular nor did his name ever appear in the newspapers; he chaired no important committee and launched no great cause; but in terms of constructive human relationships I have not known his equal. Young and old instinctively trusted him; teenagers sought him out as an understanding friend; and at the end of his life he found himself beloved by a whole community. The most attractive thing about him was his genuine unpretentiousness; he would have been astonished to the point of bewilderment to know that he had been singled out as an example of one who mirrored the Christ in whom his life was grounded. But the unheralded saint who does justice, loves mercy and walks humbly with his God may have accomplished something of far more importance and lasting worth than those who deservedly catch the public eye.

These are a few of the people I met in my early years, the memory of whom has enriched my life as I have grown older and now represents an important part of my treasure store as an octogenarian. This is supplemented by many others, most of whom are associated with the forty years during which I was married to Marjory Tait: the third decisive event which was to shape the future course of my life.

We met for the first time at the barrier of Victoria Station to catch the boat train for Switzerland in July 1946. This was a country in which I had spent more than one holiday before the war and once hostilities were over it was my ambition to go back as soon as possible. I had, therefore, arranged a small party of friends to go there, and my cousin had persuaded Marjory to join them at the last moment when one of their number had been compelled to drop out. We travelled to the Bernese Oberland by way of Spiez, but by the time we had reached the Lauterbrunnen valley I had fallen in love with Marjory and proposed to her in that idyllic setting. A picture of the Jungfrau, the Eiger and the Monch, with the snow-capped Silberhorn—my favourite mountain—hangs on the wall beside my desk as I write, bringing back memories of that holiday and especially of Marjory, with whom my life was to be so happily entwined for the next forty years.

My marriage to Marjory was to introduce me to a new circle of family and friends, as well as to the beautiful Surrey villages of Chiddingfold and Dunsfold where her father and mother lived. The roots of the family were in Scotland, where her grandfather had been Lord Provost of Glasgow and a prominent businessman, inventor and developer of the Acme wringer. Marjory's father, 'Jimmy' Tait, was chairman of Hamptons in Pall Mall and had taken over the exhibition hall of Olympia during the war to make the camouflage equipment for the invasion of Europe. He was a businessman of sterling integrity, respected by all who worked for him, whose character was exemplified by his refusal to allow his wife to use his car in wartime for anything except official business. Their only son, Ian, an officer in the Scots Guards, had been killed in action on the Anzio beachhead, but they had faced their loss with a fortitude that was typical of them. It was into their family circle that I was privileged to be welcomed.

I was also introduced to another circle of people who enlarged my horizons and added to the store of memories which has been built into my old age. They were the friends of Jimmy and Jenny Tait, among whom were General Sir Claud and Lady Liardet. He was a colourful character who had commanded the forces defending the coast of south-east England during the Battle of Britain, and he had a host of stories which were a constant source of entertainment when Marjory and I visited Chiddingfold on the days we were able to snatch as breaks from the Mission at West Ham. We enjoyed this change of scene, though Marjory was more at home with the people who made up our East London community. She had a natural aptitude for making friends with everyone and was the perfect partner in a variety of situations throughout our life together.

The end of the war brought the opportunity for travel and storing up the memory of many different countries and places. I have already mentioned the visit to Switzerland in 1946, a country to which I have often returned and which remains for me the most beautiful place in the world. Shortly after that memorable holiday on which I met and fell in love with Marjory, I paid my first visit to North America under the auspices of the British Council of Churches, preaching and lecturing in churches and colleges in Canada and on the eastern seaboard as far south as Miami. I flew across the Atlantic in a converted Lancaster bomber, touching down at

Goose Bay in Labrador, where I saw my first piece of white bread for over seven years.

Subsequently, Marjory and I were unexpectedly to make our home in Canada for twelve years when I accepted the appointment to the faculty of McMaster University in Hamilton, Ontario. This gave us the opportunity of exploring the whole continent, including a memorable trip by train from Chicago to Los Angeles via the Grand Canyon and thence by way of San Francisco and Seattle to Vancouver and Victoria. The return journey was by the Canadian Pacific Railway to Montreal through the magnificent scenery of the Canadian Rockies and the unimaginably vast prairies and northern forests.

The return to England to take up the appointment of President of the Selly Oak Colleges in Birmingham opened up a new and greatly enlarged vista, since we were responsible for the training of students going to and coming from almost every country in the world. We never had less than fifty countries represented on the campus at any one time. This entailed frequent visits to Scandinavia and Germany, from which students going to the developing countries came to us to learn English as a basic language which they were going to need for their work. Through our involvement in the world-wide missionary movement, my journeys took me to Rome, Beirut, Hong Kong, Bombay and Bangalore in South India. In 1976 I was given a sabbatical leave for three months to visit, with Marjory, centres of training in Central and South America. This gave us a picture of the instability of that part of the world, and the flagrant injustice which forced millions of our fellow human beings to live in squalid conditions of dire poverty.

These are inevitably a random selection of events, places and people which give some clue to the rich storehouse of memory on which I can look back in old age. Each of them conjures up a vast range of associations which weave the thread of memory extending over the years. Each person has his or her own treasure store, and this enables us as we grow old to evaluate the past with a mixture of gratitude and regret.

All this reminiscing should not lead to nostalgia; it should help us to look to the future, not only to reunion in another world with those whom we have loved and lost awhile, but to a constructive attitude to whatever remains of our own old age.

For Christians this is focused in an act of remembrance which has profound significance not only for the passing moment, but also for all that lies ahead in the future. When they celebrate the Last Supper, whether they call it Holy Communion, the Eucharist or the Mass, in the breaking of bread and the blessing of the cup of wine they are responding to the command of Jesus, 'Do this in remembrance of me.' This is rightly interpreted as bringing the past into the present, making available to those who receive Communion the presence of the risen Christ and all the benefits he has brought us through his suffering and death. That may at first be hard for many people to grasp, but it is the experience of Christians of all traditions. It gives a new dimension to remembering, which immeasurably enriches old age and undergirds much that I shall say in the following chapters. But, for each of us, the past has never been buried. It lives on in the contribution it has made and continues to make to our life in the present, and can be redeemed as well as fulfilled in all that lies ahead.

Chapter Four

Reflections on Experience

It has been said that the first inscription discovered by archaeologists read, when deciphered, 'Children are not what they were in my young days!' Although this must be apocryphal, it illustrates the danger from which people suffer as they grow older, by looking back on their past through rose-tinted spectacles and indulging in unjustified nostalgia. It also reflects the tendency to resist change and refrain from thinking creatively about the future. That is why the young so often write off those who are older than themselves and imagine they are out of touch with the modern world.

Although indulgence in memory can lead to unrealistic nostalgia and lack of hope for the future, this need not be so. I have known many old people who were far more radical and forward-looking than those who think that the passing fashion or craze is the touchstone by which everybody and everything should be judged.

Memory provides the material for mature reflection, for assessing what is of abiding value and for facing the future with realistic hope. In this we have much to learn from the Chinese, who venerate old age as the repository of wisdom. I am told that in China it has not been regarded as a compliment to congratulate anybody on looking younger than they are! It has been claimed that in the exercise of the higher mental processes, in comprehension, reasoning and judgment, age alone can develop, through year after year of practice, the qualities of broad objectivity. That was the view of the ancient Hebrew sage when he wrote:

Sound judgement sits well on grey hairs and wise advice comes from older men. Wisdom is fitting in the aged, and ripe counsel in men of eminence. Long experience is the old man's crown, and his pride is the fear of the Lord.[1]

Of course, wisdom is not necessarily the prerogative of old age; we may become more empty-headed and foolish as the years pass, and I would certainly not exempt myself from severe limitations and fallibility of judgment. Indeed, the older one grows, the more one becomes conscious of how little one knows, and perhaps that is the beginning of wisdom.

However, old age does afford the opportunity for more mature reflection than can be claimed for earlier years. I am, therefore, encouraged to look back and try to assess what I have found to be of value and what lessons can be learnt from it about the way ahead. Growing older has convinced me that the ideals which have been so widely adopted in both public and private life have undermined and overridden the only values of enduring worth, which are closed to those who are preoccupied with the trivialities of the passing show. Cherishing enduring values is the prerequisite of a satisfying old age, as well as of hope for the future.

As time has passed, the accumulation and preservation of *things* have come to assume less and less importance. In his autobiography Dr Eric Mascall, the noted Anglo-Catholic theologian, refers to a book he wrote many years ago in which he argued that:

> there are four orders of being: God, Man, Things and Money; and that each exists for the one before: Man for the glory of God, Things for the good of Man, Money for the production and distribution of Things. However... with man's modern repudiation of the supremacy of God, the whole scheme has not just lost its first member but has gone entirely into reverse: Things

*are for the production of Money; Man is for the
production and consumption of Things; and a very
hypothetical God is for the convenience of Man.*[2]

This seems to me to be an admirable summary of the distortion of economic priorities which has bedevilled the whole of Western economy.

We spend our lives accumulating possessions which we will leave behind us and most of which will be of little or no interest to those who come after us. Even more evanescent is the accumulation of money, which has become the goal of many of our contemporaries - though in comparative terms it has been outside the range of the vast majority, for whom an adequate pension is the most they can expect to acquire, although it will inevitably disappear on their death.

The quest for money has become a disease which has infected a high proportion of the population and eaten like a cancer at the heart of Western society. It encourages greed in the individual and injustice in society and therefore corrupts the quality of life, replacing quantity for quality in the estimation of true human values. Making the accumulation of money the goal of human endeavour obscures the way in which the real economy of material resources and human productivity can be organized to improve the welfare of the population as a whole. Money is of no value in itself; it is simply the symbol of the power to do certain things. As long as it is regarded as having value in itself, it will make the rational choice of social priorities extremely difficult, if not impossible. 'What does it profit a man if he gains the whole world and loses or forfeits himself?' said Jesus[3], and this is a question pertinently addressed to members of any society. It was underlined by what Jesus added about the man who built larger and larger barns to store his possessions: 'Fool, this night your soul is required of you; and the things you have prepared, whose will they be?'[4] Not only will he have missed what can make his life on earth of any value, but he will go empty-handed into the life beyond death.

Such a re-evaluation of money and possessions questions the assumptions of economists, politicians, industrialists and ordinary men and women alike. To replace the production of what can be quantified by that which contributes to the *quality* of the life of the individual and the community may well be regarded as unrealistic and running contrary to the natural inclinations and aspirations of human beings. But failure to do so results in what is increasingly regarded as the unacceptable face of contemporary Western society: the cult of greed and acquisitiveness, the exploitation of other people for personal gain, the obscene gap between the very rich and very poor, the rising crime rate, the drug problem, and the prevalence of violence, hooliganism and pornography. The fact that there are widespread demands for tackling these problems shows the confusion between materialistic standards and moral values.

The materialism of our society can be seen in the way in which the essential meaning of Christmas is becoming increasingly submerged by flagrant commercialization. Charles Dickens captured its true spirit in his famous classic *A Christmas Carol*, in which the old miser, Scrooge, discovers all his material wealth to be worthless when compared with the family life of his impoverished clerk. The story ends with Scrooge's celebration of Christmas with the nephew whose friendship he had previously spurned. In old age it is not the quantity of food and drink and the number of presents that matters, but the opportunity to spend the day with family and friends; and, when the circle is diminished, good neighbours and the members of the community with which we are associated help to fill the gap.

If people and their relationships alone are of enduring and ultimate worth, the values which we have come to take for granted in modern society are to be judged in the light of their contribution to that end. Besides the materialism to which I have referred, there are other shibboleths which need to be exposed and brought under critical review. The most obvious of these is the individualism which has been widely advocated and the interpretation of freedom which has been associated with it. Freedom is commonly understood in *negative* terms as the absence of restraint and the right of the individual to pursue his or her own interests unhindered by the demands of the state. This has led to the contemporary emphasis on the defence of human rights, often at the expense of promoting mutual responsibility. Freedom does, of course, entail liberation from the oppression and exploitation of which we have seen all too many examples in the modern world; but it is not properly defined until it includes the *positive* content of that for which human beings are set free—mutual responsibility in contributing to a creative community. We are not fully human if left to ourselves in isolation to pursue our own private interests. Yet this seems to be the ideal which many people have been encouraged to set before themselves. Freedom becomes licence when it is exercised at the expense of others.

However, emphasis on the importance of human relationships and the creation of genuine community is often vitiated by the all too common tendency to exclusivism in the selection of those to whom we are meaningfully related. We naturally gravitate towards those like ourselves and we are reluctant to admit into the circle of our friendship and concern those whose culture and lifestyle are other than our own. We do not like folk to be different from ourselves, and when we are confronted with the 'aliens in our midst', we try to avoid them or make them conform to our own patterns. This is at the root of the racial and ethnic prejudice and discrimination which have to be faced if we are to build a multi-racial and pluralist society. A long life, and coming to know and appreciate a great variety of people of many cultural and ethnic backgrounds, have convinced me that differences are to be welcomed, and that their acceptance is the mark of a healthy and mature society.

There are two other major convictions which have taken root and been confirmed as I reflect on the experience of having lived through the turbulent years and rapid social change of the twentieth century. The first of these is the obvious one: that war and violence are self-defeating and destructive of human values. They represent futile attempts to secure political and economic ends ultimately unobtainable by the use of force, and result in the self-destruction of those who are motivated by irrational ambition and untold suffering for ordinary people.

Many do not appear to have learned the lessons of the two world wars in this century, and still persist, as in the former Yugoslavia, in trying to achieve territorial and political advantage by force of arms. Nor does oppression, even if it seems to secure the dominance of dictatorial rulers for a time, bring lasting benefit to those who resort to it, much less to those who are its victims. The collapse of the Nazi tyranny should be sufficient evidence of that, and the Bolshevik revolution in Russia had the seeds of decay embedded in it, confounding the expectations of all those who believed it offered the promise of a better future for the human race under the banner of Marxist-Leninism. Violent revolutionaries and terrorists threaten misery and destruction to themselves as well as to their victims. The words of Jesus, 'All who take the sword will perish by the sword'[5] are amply borne out by history and underlined by the conflicts of the twentieth century.

Hope for the immediate and long-term future lies with the peacemakers, but there seems to be little evidence that their efforts will prevail and avoid catastrophes, even on a limited scale. I shall return to this subject in a later chapter when I discuss hope for the future. Here I simply want to make the point that war and violence are manifestly destructive of human values, whereas concern for the welfare of individual men, women and children and the building of genuine communities are the goals for which we should all be striving.

Most people would endorse this conclusion out of their own experience, however problematic they might think it to be in the kind of world in which we are living. But my other main conclusion as I reflect on past experience is likely to be much more controversial. It is that the type of confrontation politics to which we have become accustomed and which is embedded in our most cherished institutions is inappropriate for facing the problems of the next millennium. The last century has been marked by quite bewildering scientific and technological developments. The world has become what has been called 'a global village'. In other words, modern methods of travel and communication, taken together with the international organization of trade and finance, have rendered the nation state obsolete as a self-sufficient unit. Many of the major governmental decisions which affect our lives have to be taken on a transnational basis, and it is simply burying our heads in the sand to suppose that traditional notions of national sovereignty apply in a world which has outgrown them.

This is the issue at stake in the heated debates about the future development of the European Community. Business people and industrialists have come to recognize that major economic decisions have to be taken by securing agreements on an international basis. Politicians, on the other hand, feel threatened when they see power being transferred to the administration in Brussels and the European parliament in Strasbourg. Beyond this is the wider international organization of the United Nations which will increasingly have to take responsibility for keeping the peace and dealing with what are essentially global problems: the conservation of the environment and the regulation of health standards and economic development, for example.

The major political question for the future has nothing to do with the preservation of national sovereignty, which has already begun to be irrevocably abandoned, but with the distribution of power. The issue we now have to face is one of who does what best; at what level does agreement on matters of policy have to be reached? This means deciding what questions are most effectively dealt with on an international, European, national, regional or local level. Most ordinary people are mainly concerned with those matters which affect their families and the organizations to which they belong in their local community. As far as possible these questions should be remitted to genuinely local government, in which they can participate. But very many decisions which affect their daily lives have to be taken by representatives at higher levels of government, who are elected to serve in their interests. Trust in the instruments of government, however, has largely broken down, and we now face the problem that an increasing proportion of the electorate are alienated from the existing political process.

The radical reformation of parliamentary and local government which is going to be necessary to meet the needs of the future is undoubtedly going to be threatening to politicians wedded to traditional ways of conducting public affairs. It will mean surrendering powers in one direction to international agencies and in another to regional and local instruments of government, retaining only what is appropriate to an elected national assembly. This certainly means establishing the principle of subsidiarity: that no decision should be taken at a higher level than is absolutely necessary, and that detailed regulations are not imposed on the lower levels of government.

Of course, this means abandoning the traditional party game of confrontation between the Right and the Left: the adversarial politics which have increasingly fallen into public disfavour. They now need to be replaced by those inter-party and inter-governmental compromises and agreements which have necessarily been the feature of European and United Nations jurisdiction, and which are clearly emerging as the most satisfactory form of regional and local government.

Surrendering or, more positively, sharing power will be the most difficult political nettle to grasp over the coming years; for politicians, like most people, do not like to face change and they are reluctant to see power slipping away through their fingers. Moreover, the deep emotions will be evoked which come to the fore at times of national celebration such as that marking the anniversary of VE Day in Europe. But British parliamentarians are being slow to acknowledge that their confrontational behaviour, depicted vividly on television screens and on the radio, lies behind much of the modern distaste for politicians and politics, and that the general public are coming to appreciate alliances and coalitions where they are beginning to experience them in local government. Those who have a vested interest in the political power game as it has been played for the last two hundred years or more will resist any change, but the way in which power is shared is long overdue for radical review in the interests of the welfare and concerns of ordinary people.

Disillusionment with the current political process has led many people, mistakenly as I believe, to opt out of their electoral responsibilities, refusing to vote for anyone at all. For some time the impression has been gaining ground that the way we vote at both national and local elections makes no difference to the way we are governed. This attitude is not always an abdication of civic responsibility. A growing number, particularly of the young, believe that the only way in which wrongs can be righted and real change effected is by joining one of the many pressure groups which campaign for a variety of causes, notably for the protection of the environment, the defence of animal rights, and the welfare of homeless, unemployed, disadvantaged and handicapped people.

The significance of these pressure groups is that many people feel that they can identify with them in a way that is not possible by joining a political party, which seems to them to be fossilized in power structures over which they can have no influence. This view may be mistaken, but politicians of all parties need to take it seriously and understand that the great majority of people only feel involved in the families, groups and voluntary associations which constitute the neighbourhood and community of which they are a part. For example, Rotary Clubs, the Inner Wheel, or local organizations for promoting all kinds of hobbies and interests are far more important to them than than political parties; for within them they can make friends and establish their identity.

At first sight, it may appear that my reflection on the materialism, intolerance, violence and confrontational politics that have characterized society in the twentieth century has been a diversion from the subject of this book. But growing older has convinced me that the values which have come to dominate the Western world have led to nothing but misery and frustration, and that the achievements of enduring worth are those which have contributed to constructive human relationships. It is these which we may look back on with gratitude in old age and seek to foster in whatever time is still allotted to us. The important things in life are not those that capture the headlines in the press, but those that involve our relationships with other people. In his widely acclaimed book *Christianity and History*, the Cambridge historian Herbert Butterfield wrote: 'Those people work more wisely who seek to achieve good in their own small corner of the world and then leave the leaven to leaven the whole lump, than those who are for ever thinking that life is vain unless one can act through central government, carry legislation, achieve political power and do big things.'[6] Old age may put the present, no less than the past, into perspective.

Chapter Five

The Problem of Loneliness

If we are to sustain the argument that the prospect of old age is one of an expanding future in which human relationships prove to be of enduring value, we have to face the problems inherent in ageing which seem to make such a thesis untenable. Loneliness is one of the most obvious of these, affecting an increasing number of our fellow citizens. It follows inevitably from the gradual loss of relatives, friends and even acquaintances, and the circle gets smaller as the years pass, ending up in virtual isolation for many elderly people.

To some extent the problem is mitigated for those who have been married and have produced a family. The coming of grandchildren, with the interest in their growth and development, adds immeasurably to the joys of old age. The family circle may even become further enlarged as they grow up and are married themselves, producing another generation of great-grandchildren.

The extended family, although it has not been such a fundamental and widespread bond in constituting the basis of Western society as it has been, for example, on the African continent, has nevertheless played a significant part in shaping our way of life. Some of the older generation may remember *Dear Octopus*, the stage play by Dodie Smith in which Dame Marie Tempest played the part of the beloved grandmother around whom the family circled and who was the focus of reconciliation in times of crisis.

If the play were to be revived today, most theatre-goers would regard it as old-fashioned, out of tune with the contemporary scene. For very many people, of course, the family is still the bulwark of society, but it is generally a smaller unit than it used to be. In Victorian and Edwardian times families of ten or more children were common, but now most parents do not expect to have more than two or three. Such has been the result of modern methods of birth control, coupled with the economic and social pressures of women going out to work. The typical role of the mother of a family has changed dramatically, particularly since the end of the Second World War.

Despite the continuing place of the family in the

life of the nation and the lip service paid to its importance as the building block of a healthy society, we have hardly come to terms as yet with the striking changes that have taken place in the popular conception of marriage, home and family over the past century, culminating in the increasing number of casual relationships, divorces and single-parent families. Since the dawn of the industrial revolution family ties in Great Britain have been gradually weakened. In olden days the village community was the basis of a stable social life for most people, with families intermarrying and living together in the same place from birth to death. But migration to the towns in search of work in the new factories transformed the face of Britain, with the ultimate growth of huge conurbations in which people have come to lose their sense of identity and their feeling of belonging to one another.

Before the Second World War the comradeship of the street was the bond which held many families together. The development of housing estates, however, and particularly the building of high-rise tower blocks, have broken down any sense of community and created the feeling of isolation even for families, let alone for single people. The comment of the old lady that she had been buried alive seven storeys above the ground is a devastating judgment on the mistakes of post-war planners who failed to take into account the social implications of rebuilding the bombed sites of our major cities. Many of these tower blocks, erected at huge expense only a few years ago, are having to be demolished because they have been vandalized and because people refuse to live in them any longer. This is sufficient commentary on the folly of neglecting the way people are related to one another in the interests of the supposed economies of space and finance. The post-war planners and the architects whom they instructed carry a heavy responsibility for the growing problem of loneliness which is afflicting modern society.

This sense of isolation is not restricted to people living in blocks of flats, although that type of accommodation encourages a feeling of anonymity and results in residents becoming numbers in the address or rent book instead of neighbours. When in the 1950s I was sent by my university in Canada on a tour of exploration in North America and Europe to see what student residences and union facilities were being planned for the future, one of the locations I visited was in the state of New York where I was shown the latest tower block to be built. The administrator told me that a week or so previously a student had committed suicide by throwing himself out of a window on the eleventh floor and, when the police investigated the tragedy, they could find nobody in the residence who knew him!

But loneliness may not be due simply to this type of isolation. It may have its roots in introversion or a lack of self-confidence which has made relationships with other people difficult, and this may build up over the years. Perhaps the greatest fear of many men and women as they grow older is that they will no longer be wanted by anyone. When the head of a sociology department presented a questionnaire to a large number of people of all ages, she found that the younger ones thought that when they reached the age of seventy they would most want financial security and freedom from responsibility, whereas older people invariably headed their list with the desire to be loved, wanted and useful.

The family has been, and still is, the main bulwark against loneliness and the fear of not being wanted in old age. But this is not always so. When children grow up, move away, get married and set up their own homes, families become scattered, and the old people are left to fend for themselves. Sometimes they move to be near their children, but this is not always possible; sons and daughters change their jobs and in our highly mobile society cannot be counted on to provide an anchorage in any locality for their parents. In any case, too close proximity can be a cause of friction, for old people can be very demanding. That is why it is generally wise for them not to go and live in the home of their son or daughter. They need their own independence as well as to respect that of the younger members of their family circle. A balance has to be struck between supportive family relationships and freedom to enjoy a proper independence.

All the same, a loving family can be the context within which life may be progressively enriched and in which the fear of not being wanted and reduced to loneliness in old age ceases to be a menacing prospect. Unhappily, that is not the good fortune of a growing number of people in our society who lack the support of a family, either through choice in adopting a single life or because circumstances have given them no option. Their number has dramatically increased over recent years and it is estimated that the figure has been growing by 120,000 a year, reaching approximately six million by the end of the 1980s. Many of these, mostly women, might have chosen to get married and raise a family if they had found a partner. Then there is the increasing number of divorcees and single parents. In many cases the latter are not living alone since they continue to have the care of children, but they are deprived of the support of a partner in making a home and this can be a very lonely burden.

To some extent friends compensate for the lack of committed partners, but a great many face increasing loneliness in old age. The total of single people is swollen by the growing percentage of the elderly in our population, many of them widows and widowers, who find themselves housebound and unable to care for themselves as once they did. It is with them that we are particularly concerned in this book, whether their loneliness is due to the pattern of life they have chosen or been forced to adopt in earlier years, or is the inevitable result of the loss of partners, relatives and friends.

Of course, there are a great many who have deliberately chosen the single life, either to pursue an independent career or because they do not want to assume the responsibility of marriage and a family. It is perfectly justifiable for them to claim that this is a legitimate option and in no way implies a second class role in society. That is widely recognized by men and has only been downgraded as far as women are concerned because of the age-old assumption that marriage and home-making are a woman's natural function. Feminists are right to protest against this, though in defending their case some of them seem insensitive to those of their own sex whose aspirations are different from their own.

We have to recognize that marriage, though a crucially important constituent of a healthy society, is not for everyone. The single life, whatever form it may take, can be the means to personal fulfilment and should not be depreciated in favour of the married state. Both have their rewards as well as their problems. Many who embark on marriage are not fitted for it, temperamentally or because of upbringing or natural inclination. They find this out for themselves, often through bitter experience. It is an art, fraught with pitfalls and difficulty, which has to be learnt. Often when the initial romance has worn off and mutual physical attraction has lost its appeal, husband and wife find it hard to adjust to the differences between them. Instead of sharing their interests and encouraging one another to fulfil their respective aspirations, they become irritated with each other and gradually drift apart. The marriage, even if it lasts for a long time, becomes progressively drab and unsatisfying. Sometimes a second marriage proves more successful when people learn from experience, but many more find that they are simply unable to cope with this kind of relationship; they should never have been married in the first place.

But the single life is not an easy option and can store up problems for old age unless a range of interests and a widening circle of friends characterize this lifestyle. Some of the most successful women and men who become absorbed in their jobs or professions find themselves completely bereft on retirement, at a loss for something to do and having had no time to forge any lasting relationships. The prospect of loneliness is also enhanced by the spread of sexual permissiveness in contemporary society, which places a premium on promiscuity and casual relationships, undermining the capacity to make the close friendships which are of such importance as the years pass. The encouragement of individualism at the expense of community involvement and the development of a sense of responsibility for other people store up problems not only for society at large, but for many who opt for the single life.

If this is accepted, it is clear why loneliness is the major problem confronting single people, especially as they grow older. We are made for community and we are what we are and what we become only in relationship to other people. Children are naturally gregarious; they look for friends with whom to play; the lonely and neglected child is a sad spectacle. Teenagers join gangs, often for destructive purposes when they are bored, or try to establish their own identity by associating with their peers. This, not poverty or unemployment, is the underlying reason for hooliganism on the football terraces and mindless vandalism and violence in run-down urban areas. The fact that this phenomenon is spreading to small towns and even the countryside should make us hesitate before offering too facile solutions to the problem. Unless young people are afforded the opportunity to belong to a constructive community they will grow up lacking the capacity for healthy relationships with other people, and the end of that road is the most terrible frustration, isolation and loneliness in later years.

Since I retired, I have come to realize how the loss of marriage partners, friends and acquaintances progressively narrows the prospect for many old people. I have been singularly fortunate in a second marriage which has introduced me to another family and circle of friends, but it has also made me aware of the potential loneliness of many others as they have grown older. Retirement brings people into contact with those for whom the circle is a narrowing one, and the encouragement is often lacking to open new doors and make new friends of the people around them - people who may well be looking for the companionship and understanding which neighbours can supply. Overcoming loneliness is a co-operative venture which will never get off the ground without someone taking the initiative. But, in doing so, we may discover that we have gifts and experience which otherwise would remain buried. Being a good neighbour is something that even the housebound and infirm can contribute to other people, and those who take the initiative in visiting the elderly who cannot move around as once they did often find that their care is returned with interest many times over.

The Problem of Loneliness

In an earlier chapter I referred to John Keogh as one of those who stand out in my treasure store of memory. He, more than anyone else I have known, exemplified the good neighbour who did not wait to be called upon for help. After his wife died, leaving him alone in his seventies, he devoted himself to the care of anyone in need, visiting them when they were housebound, helping them with domestic chores when they were ill, and often spending the night with someone who was dying. He continued this unobtrusive ministry until he was well into his nineties, dying beloved by a whole community, not least by young teenagers who sought him out as a wise and understanding friend. He has been a constant source of inspiration to me over the years and is an outstanding example of how one elderly man claiming no special gifts or qualifications could enrich a whole community.

The problem of growing older and facing loneliness is particularly acute for single women. Men in general do not recognize the handicaps they suffer. Quite apart from having had to face the fact that they are unlikely to bear children and will not have the support of a family when they grow older, they often find themselves in a social setting geared very largely to married people. On holidays, single rooms are often difficult to obtain in hotels and boarding-houses as well as being inferior and much more expensive. More seriously, it is increasingly dangerous for them to go out alone into the streets of our cities, particularly at night, for fear of being attacked. Many older women shut themselves up in the evenings and never venture outside. Men congregate in pubs and clubs which, if not male preserves, are not particularly hospitable to women.

But loneliness is a problem which men as well as women face as they grow older. We are made for relationship with one another and the answer to the problem of loneliness is a caring community. Much has been achieved in this century through the advent of the welfare state. Not only have old age pensions become an established right of everyone over retirement age, but provisions are made for home helps and the physical care of those who are no longer able to look after themselves. As we contrast this with the poverty and deprivation of the nineteenth century, we do well to recognize the advances that have been made in social welfare and which now have to be defended against the political encroachments threatened by the cult of individual selfishness and attempts to cut back state expenditure in the interests of lower taxation. But welcome and necessary as these material provisions are, which have to be the responsibility of the state in a civilized society, they go no further than undergirding the framework for tackling the problem of loneliness in old age. This is essentially the task of the local community and is dependent upon the initiatives of voluntary organizations, such as Age Concern and Help The Aged, and more particularly upon the cultivation of neighbourliness to which I have already referred and which is the hallmark of a caring community.

Much is achieved by the establishment of day centres where senior citizens can meet one another, by clubs devoted to a variety of interests for the elderly, and by specialist companies which arrange for excursions and holidays for senior citizens. A great deal can be done for the housebound in ensuring that they are not left friendless, but are regularly visited by neighbours; and in this the encouragement of the young to take an interest in older people and help them with doing such things as gardening and shopping turns out to be for their mutual benefit. The promotion of neighbourliness is the prerequisite for retaining those who are physically and mentally handicapped in their own homes rather than compelling them to be accommodated in nursing homes at considerable expense and largely cut off from the stimulation of a mixed community.

The pain of loneliness is essentially the loss of the sense of belonging to anybody, and in counteracting this the churches have a significant part to play; for they are meant to be the family of families from which no one is excluded and where all find their place in belonging to the family of God. Unhappily this is more often maintained in theory rather than realized in practice. All too many of those who attend Roman Catholic or Anglican churches go there as individuals and scarcely speak to anyone else except for a cursory handshake with the priest at the door. The Free Churches have a somewhat better record, based on their conviction that the local congregation is the gathered community of believers, but even with them it has to be recognized that the reality of the church as a fellowship or community is often experienced by relatively few. It is easy for anyone entering any church to pass unnoticed, and this particularly applies if they are strangers who may not receive even a cursory welcome.

Of course, there are a great many exceptions, and a large number of new church buildings are designed to provide comfortable rooms and coffee bars where people can meet one another after a service and where groups of various kinds can meet during the week. But it has to be confessed that in this respect Great Britain is far behind the United States, as was vividly illustrated in a series of television programmes in 1991 which examined the state of organized religion in the British Isles. The small proportion of the population attending any of the churches in England, Scotland and Wales was contrasted with over 50 per cent on the other side of the Atlantic—sometimes greater in certain places. The explanation given was that American churches are organized to provide opportunities for people to share meals together and to engage in a wide variety of interest groups throughout the week. In Britain the common image of the church in the public mind is the corner shop: the building in the High Street presided over by a clergyman, where the rites of passage at birth, marriage and death can be celebrated, and services of worship provided for those who care to attend. The idea that the church is essentially the people of God, those committed to each other in the service of his kingdom and sharing together in a common life, is almost totally obscured by the way in which the churches have come to be structured.

If local congregations are to make the contribution which they ought to do in resolving the problem of loneliness and helping to build genuine community, more searching questions need to be asked than is generally the case. Is the local church simply an exclusive religious club for the like-minded? In a paper prepared for the assembly of the World Council of Churches in Canberra the Scottish theologian, Dr Elizabeth Templeton, asked the far-reaching question of whether the churches have signally failed to follow their Lord in welcoming everyone without conditions, including those perceived as the enemy.[1] Jesus scandalized his contemporaries by consorting with the outcasts of society, the prostitutes, the tax collectors, the poor, the disadvantaged and the ritually unclean. How is this, asked Dr Templeton, to be reconciled with fencing off the communion table, opposing indiscriminate baptism and communion, insisting on conformity in belief as a condition of acceptability or laying down rules of behaviour as a criterion of respectability? 'Love your enemies and pray for your persecutors; only so can you be children of your heavenly Father, who makes his sun rise on good and bad alike, and sends his rain on the honest and dishonest.'[2] Or again, Jesus is reported to have said, 'The man who comes to me I will never turn away.'[3]

This is the challenge to every local congregation. It needs to ask how far it is really open to everyone in the community. To put it bluntly, is it prepared to be obedient to the demands of the gospel or is it fenced to protect its own distinctiveness? The record is not a good one even amongst those congregations which claim to have taken the idea of community seriously. A survey undertaken in one denomination a few years ago of the types of provision made for people to meet in groups revealed that these were extremely limited and more often than not inward looking and restricted to those who conformed to certain patterns of commitment. Very few congregations had taken seriously the needs of the community at large.

A caring community in which everyone is welcomed and nobody excluded is the answer to the problem of loneliness at every stage of life, particularly for the elderly when they live alone. The churches have a unique opportunity as well as a clear responsibility to take the lead in meeting this need. Many will doubtless find friendship and community in other ways. But in the end the body of Christ is the model and the ultimate fulfilment of everyone, whoever they may be. There is no loneliness in the kingdom of God.

Chapter Six

Facing Infirmity

Infirmity is primarily, though not exclusively, a problem of old age. It is distinguished from specific illnesses by being defined as general organic weakness, leading to a variety of handicaps, the most common of which is impairment in mobility. Many people do not have to face this problem because they die before they become infirm. However, suffering and illness may overtake anyone at any time, and that too may be an accompaniment of infirmity. In the light of this prospect, how can it reasonably be maintained that old age can be the fulfilment of life?

The problem of suffering is one that has baffled people of every generation. It is particularly acute in relation to those who have to undergo it earlier in life; in old age it may seem to be less intractable because it is fatalistically regarded as the natural outcome of the deterioration of the physical organism. But whether it is the experience of the young or the old, it presents the theoretical problem of explaining how it can be understood as a feature of a rational universe and how in practice it is to be met and overcome.

Many books have been written on the subject from a theoretical point of view, but none of them ultimately carries conviction. It is only when anyone speaks or writes out of their own experience about battling with suffering and infirmity that they can say anything which is of much help to fellow sufferers or carries real conviction to anyone else. Dr Donald Soper, who was so successful in drawing the crowds to enjoy his masterful skill at repartee in the open air on London's Tower Hill, was once caught out when someone interrupted him by pontificating about conditions in America. Exasperated, Soper asked him whether he had ever been there. 'Well—er—no,' was the reply. To which came Soper's immediate rejoinder: 'You shouldn't claim to know anything about a place you've never visited'. Whereupon a wag in the crowd pointedly asked, 'Dr Soper, have you ever been to heaven?'

One of the best known and most influential books about the problem of pain was written by the late C.S. Lewis,[1] but it was only when he had to wrestle with the suffering and terminal cancer of the woman he married late in life that he spoke with a fresh authenticity. This was movingly portrayed in *Shadowlands*, the film which won such wide acclaim.

I was wrestling with the same problem, not only

in the light of my own wife's death after a four-year battle against cancer, but in the wake of the tragedies so many people have had to suffer at the hands of terrorists in Northern Ireland and elsewhere. If God does not meet us and come to our aid in our hour of need, the suffering is unrelieved and there is nothing more to be said. If on the other hand he is found by any individual to be 'a very present help in trouble',[2] this is potentially the case for anyone else, even in the midst of widespread disaster; for the problem is not accentuated by the scale of the suffering—in every case it is one man, one woman or one child who is the innocent victim. If only one child is killed or maimed in a terrorist attack and nobody else, that is no different from one child amidst thousands massacred in Rwanda or Burundi or one child among others murdered in the shelling of Sarajevo. Tragedy, suffering or sudden death may strike any one of us at any time, whether we be young or old, and although we may try to delude ourselves by hoping that this will not fall on us or those we love, it is a very likely prospect as we grow older.

As I wrestled with this, I found myself turning to the book of Job in the Old Testament: probably the most realistic and profound facing of the problem in the whole of the world's literature. In the first two chapters of the book Job is portrayed as an outstandingly good man who feared God and had always tried to do his will. Moreover, he had prospered and was very wealthy. Then disaster overtook him and he suffered calamity upon calamity. He lost all his possessions; his family was similarly devastated; he was the victim of all kinds of physical disease and mental torment. His life alone was spared and he wished he had never been born. He was even reduced to cursing the God who had created him and whom he had faithfully tried to serve.

Most of the rest of the poem concerns the attempts of three of his friends, Eliphaz, Bildad and Zophar, to bring him comfort. They were good men and drew on the best they knew from the Hebrew tradition, just as Christians do today out of their much richer heritage. The three friends trotted out the familiar argument that Job's sufferings must be due to his sin—very like the argument advanced by some Christians that natural disasters as well as moral evil are attributable to the primordial fall of man. A similar assumption was made by the disciples of Jesus when they asked him about a blind man, 'Who sinned, this man or his parents, that he was born blind?'[3]

The argument of his friends does not satisfy Job. He replies that the wicked and those who defy God often enjoy prosperity until the day of their death, and becomes more and more angry with them as he feels they are not meeting his own problem. Towards the end of the poem a wise old man, Elihu, who has been listening in silence to the argument, tries another tack. If only Job would be patient, all would work out well in the end. This makes Job even more frustrated.

At last he realizes that no one else can help him; he must find the answer for himself. Now he is addressed directly by God, who does not speak about the suffering of the innocent either in general or in Job's particular case. He confronts him with the wonders of his creation, overwhelming Job with his majesty and his glory. This at last reduces the sufferer to acknowledge his own impotence and utter dependence on the Lord, and he ends by confessing:

I know that thou canst do all things
and that no purpose is beyond thee.
But I have spoken of great things which I have not
understood,
things too wonderful for me to know.
I knew of thee only by report,
but now I see thee with my own eyes.
Therefore I melt away;
I repent in dust and ashes.[4]

Jesus gave essentially the same answer to his disciples about the man born blind: he was born blind 'that the works of God might be made manifest in him'.[5] And the power and glory of God was paradoxically revealed beyond anything that could have been conceived by the author of the book of Job in the suffering and death of Jesus himself, so that the writer of the Epistle to the Hebrews could say, 'Since he himself has passed through the test of suffering, he is able to help those who are meeting their test now.'[6]

This is no armchair or academic solution to the problem of evil and suffering. It leads to the conclusion that only the sufferer can find the answer for himself or herself in a personal encounter with God. Nobody else can do so, even those who are closest to them. And this has happened frequently, as many people can testify. When the news was full of the outrages committed by terrorists in Northern Ireland, I was deeply moved by the way in which Gordon Wilson responded to the murder of his daughter at the war memorial in Enniskillen, which was followed some months later by a similar reaction on the part of Roman Catholics to the atrocity in the village of Greysteel. Instead of reacting with hatred and bitterness they seemed to have discovered God, not only sharing their suffering but enabling them to overcome it. Nobody is entitled to claim from a detached and theoretical point of view that the problem of suffering is insoluble and defies any ultimate meaning when they are faced with the testimony of those who have passed through the 'valley of the shadow of death' and who have found their faith in God and their experience of his present help strengthened thereby.

Of course, there are many who have found little or no comfort in the tragedies that have overtaken them, but that does not nullify the fact that there is powerful testimony to the resources in God which are available to those who turn to him and find that he shares their sufferings and has achieved their redemption. As Dietrich Bonhoeffer wrote from prison when he faced execution at the hands of the Nazis, 'Only a suffering God can help.' That does not solve the theoretical problem, but it shows that sceptical dogmatism does not have the last word.

I have not had to suffer the pain and tragedy which many others have had to endure, but I have experienced illness and infirmity in which I have discovered the same kind of assurance as that to which I have referred above. On the whole I have enjoyed a very healthy and active life and, although I have been privileged to hold positions of fascinating responsibility, I have found the years of retirement since 1979 the most interesting and stimulating period of my life. However, more recently I began to suffer from a variety of illnesses and a year later started to have difficulty with walking. The condition deteriorated until just before Christmas in 1992 I underwent an operation on the nerves at the back of my neck which had become compressed and were inhibiting the movement of the left leg. The surgeon explained that, although he hoped he had prevented the problem from getting worse, it would be a bonus if there was any improvement, and he gave me a year to see if this would happen. It did not, and so here I am, dependent on a zimmer for being able to move around our little flat and a wheelchair for greater distances. In this I share the handicap to which many people have to adjust much earlier in their lives.

This disability, of course, prevents me from doing many of the things I previously enjoyed; freedom to travel and go for walks in the beautiful countryside. It inhibits a whole range of activities like being able to use my hands when I am on my feet and makes me dependent on someone else to fetch and carry the things I need. But there are many compensations, such as more time for reflection, reading and writing, and still more for learning dependence on other people and discovering how kind and helpful others can be when they see you need assistance.

This may seem a strange claim to those who cherish their independence and delude themselves into thinking that character is formed only by developing their own inner resources. I learnt how mistaken such an attitude could be from a serious illness which confined me to a hospital bed just over eighteen months ago. For the first fortnight I was so ill that I thought I was going to die. I was unable to move in the bed without assistance and I could not even feed myself. I was utterly helpless and entirely dependent on my wife, the doctors and the nurses for that short time until I began gradually to recover and regain my strength. The greatest contribution was made by the hospital chaplain whose sacramental ministry assured me of my ultimate dependence on God. This was a profound spiritual experience for which I was deeply grateful, confirming something I suppose I had always instinctively known: that pride in one's own abilities to cope with life is an illusion and that we are from first to last dependent on one another and ultimately on God. Henley's much quoted lines, 'I am the master of my fate; I am the captain of my soul'[7] are not the acme of heroism, but the pathetic nadir of human delusion. Abraham Lincoln may not be typical of the world's statesmen, but he had discovered his limitations when he said, 'I have been driven many times to my knees by the overwhelming conviction that I had nowhere else to go; my own wisdom and that of all around me seemed insufficient for the day.' That is the most important discovery of old age, crystallized by illness and infirmity.

I have already referred to the loving care which may be experienced by those who are stricken with illness and infirmity in old age. It is perhaps the most rewarding characteristic of a mature and healthy community: rewarding not only for the beneficiaries and recipients, but also for those who are able to find a vocation in contributing to it. Community care is now a dominant feature of public policy, but too often in practice it is restricted to the provision of material welfare (though this is sorely lacking in much of the provision for the homeless as well as for those who are physically and mentally handicapped). Far more important is the loving care of neighbours and friends and, when medical help is required, the sensitive and compassionate treatment which makes illness and infirmity easier to bear and smooths the way to a peaceful ending of life's journey.

I shall have more to say about this in the next chapter when we come to the subject of dying. But in the meantime something more needs to be said about facing sickness and infirmity and the help which can be given to us when we are patients.

Tremendous advances have been made in medical science during the last century. Cures have been found for a number of diseases; the techniques for treating serious illnesses have been immeasurably improved and drugs have been invented which prolong life far beyond the age of retirement;

antibiotics and resuscitation procedures have enabled the medical profession to keep patients alive when in former days they would almost certainly have died. Furthermore, the control of pain has now reached a stage at which needless suffering can be prevented. These achievements have revolutionized the treatment of illness and progress in medical research is being made all the time.

But it is questionable whether the care of patients has improved in pace with scientific and technological advances. This is not altogether surprising since scientific interest tends to concentrate on objects rather than persons, and patients can then be treated as bodies to be mended rather than as people to be healed. The problem has been compounded in Britain over the past twenty years by changes in the administration of the National Health Service in which lay administrators have been introduced into hospitals, the former hierarchy of nursing care of matrons and sisters replaced by those whose primary remit seems to be the manipulation of statistics and measures dictated by financial economy. The ethos of the management of Shell Oil may be appropriate to the conduct of a vast business enterprise, but it is disastrous when applied to the administration of a caring service. Citing the numbers treated as if this was a criterion of success, without attention being given to the quality of service provided, is treating patients like units in a sausage machine.

Of course, generalizations can be faulted and are always open to contradiction. Some parts of the NHS exceed the highest hopes the pioneers had for it, and many patients, of whom I am one, have reason to be profoundly grateful and appreciative of the treatment they have received. But that is not uniformally the case. Nobody can doubt that all is far from well in this vast organization, and demands for pouring even more money into it are no remedy for what is wrong. The real trouble lies in the way the NHS is administered, the criteria which govern decisions about the allocation of resources, and the education and training of nurses.

Morale in the hospital nursing service is low, and this is not simply due to dissatisfaction about pay awards. The patient's own perception of the way he or she is treated is very different from that of most administrators. I write from the background of a good deal of experience as a patient in recent years, from my observation of the way in which others are treated, and from my knowledge of a number of retired senior nurses who are deeply disturbed about the marked deterioration in the quality of care and supervision that is now a widespread feature of the NHS. Moreover, there are many in the medical profession today who fear that the introduction of

Project 2000, which looks to the major part of nursing education being transferred to colleges, will lead to an even more rapid decline.

The reason for this is that training nurses to be 'technical medical assistants' destroys the concept developed since the days of Florence Nightingale of establishing a strong and independent professional body, dedicated to supporting the medical profession in all aspects of its work and uniquely caring for the patients in ways that are essential to their comfort and recovery. To remove the major part of nursing training from the 'patient areas' into technical colleges can only accelerate the current deterioration of care in many wards. Nursing is an art, not a science, and the art of relating compassionately to anxious and sick people is more difficult to acquire than technological competence.

The traditional responsibility of ward sisters under the matron for the leadership and supervision of a team has been further undermined by the introduction of 'housekeeping' staff—to serve meals to patients, for example—and the overall impression of a lack of cohesion in ward management. In many cases, therefore, patients feel that there is inadequate staff supervision. I have seen trays delivered out of the reach of very sick patients and removed untouched without anyone appearing to notice.

Anyone who has been a patient can see the result

of inappropriate administration in understaffed wards, and nurses who appear never to have been taught how to treat and care for the sick and elderly. Their comfort in bed, the way they are fed and, above everything else, the comforting reassurance of an understanding relationship are far more important than a theoretical knowledge of scientific diagnosis, which is the province of the doctors. On one occasion when a complaint was lodged about the inadequate staffing of a ward, its lack of proper supervision and the attitude of nurses to patients, the administrator's response was that this would be referred to the floor manager! The terminology used indicates the heart of the problem.

I have dwelt in some detail with hospital deficiencies in the National Health Service because nearly all old people have the experience of admission to a sick bay at one time or another and many have to end their journey on earth there. Statistical targets are no substitute for compassionate care. Much more could be said along the same lines about the social services and care in the community. Those who have responsibility for ministering to the needs of the sick and the weak have a very difficult task in establishing the right kind of relationship, and many are incapable of doing so because of their preoccupation with their own problems. I have known nurses with unhappy love affairs or broken marriages who have simply taken out their frustrations and misery on their patients. Of course, it works the other way round as well. Many old people can be cantankerous and impossibly demanding. Relationship is a two-way affair. That is not always appreciated. The carer, whether a nurse or a social worker or even a friendly neighbour, may benefit even more from a good relationship than the patient or client or the handicapped person next door. If building personal relationships and community are the enduring values, everyone on both the giving and the receiving ends is ultimately a beneficiary.

This cannot be sufficiently stressed. The improvement of the Health and Social Services is something to which all of us have a contribution to make. Many of the defects in the caring services are due to the attitudes and expectations we bring to them. A cantankerous and demanding patient is not likely to win a sympathetic response, whereas a positive and appreciative attitude brings out the best in a carer.

Many years ago I was a patient in the Queen Elizabeth Hospital in Birmingham where I received superb nursing care during my recovery from an operation. But the wound did not heal as rapidly as expected, and I was compelled to stay in hospital for another three weeks until it did, feeling well and able to talk to my fellow patients. In contrast to the cheerfulness of the majority of the staff, there were two nurses who seemed incapable of raising a smile, and the patients in the ward suffered accordingly. I determined to get a smile out of them and establish a friendly relationship. Both of them were suffering from unhappy love affairs and that was the explanation of their attitude to everybody else. It took a week to break through their emotional resistance, but at the end of it they were able to relate more positively to some very sick and helpless patients.

Carping criticism is simply destructive and gets nowhere. Our public services are in need of reform and lifting on to a higher plane. But in all that we have a part to play. Nobody need fear illness and infirmity if they bring to it a positive attitude and look for a caring response. Helping the carers brings its own reward.

Chapter Seven

The Adventure of Dying

'Men fear death as children fear to go into the dark,' wrote Francis Bacon.[1] In what sense is that true? Do we fear death as the extinction of life here on earth or are we afraid of what may lie beyond? Or do we fear dying, the process of experiencing life ebbing away, often accompanied by pain and suffering? Although Bacon did not distinguish between death and dying, the distinction is an important one. While death is inevitable, it may be fatalistically regarded as the extinction of life altogether, to be postponed as long as possible, but not feared, provided it is not preceded by suffering. On the other hand, death may be anticipated as an adventure, into either the darkness or the light according to an individual's religious faith.

The question of what, if anything, lies beyond death will concern us in the next chapter. Here I want to concentrate on the process of dying: a prospect which awaits all of us and of which many are afraid as they grow older. Some may escape the experience by sudden and unexpected death while still enjoying the best of health, but most of us will end our days with the prelude of illness of one kind or another. Whether it be long or short, we have to be prepared for it, and it is natural that we should be fearful of the unknown. The fear of dying is like going into the dark, and we should not try to suppress our anxieties; it is much healthier to bring them into the open and learn from the experience of those who have gone before us.

Of course, it makes a world of difference to the way in which we face the prospect of dying if we do so with a firm belief in the love of God and his power to sustain us through whatever we have to suffer, and with hope of a life beyond death, compared to which life on earth is to dwell in the Shadowlands, to use C.S. Lewis's graphic image. But, whether we have this hope or not, there is much we may experience in common.

One of the most puzzling questions is whether we can have the experience of actually dying. Those who believe that death implies extinction would have to say that it is impossible, a contradiction in terms; but there are those who have been on the brink of death and have recovered to tell others what it has been like. How far this is evidence for a life beyond death is a matter of dispute to which we shall return later, but it cannot easily be dismissed as having nothing to say about the moments immediately preceding dying, and may even be interpreted as at least a glimpse of what lies beyond.

Such accounts are rare, but they often take the form of detachment from the body and observation of what surgeons and nurses are doing to it from a viewpoint above and beyond the operating table. This kind of experience is well authenticated and cannot be ignored as the fanciful imagination of the gullible. The most striking example I know is that of my former Vice-Chancellor at McMaster University. George Gilmour was one of the outstanding personalities in the educational world of Canada in the 1950s—a man endowed with a brilliant and critical mind, but a body that would not stand the pace at which he was living. He died at a comparatively early age, but a year or so before heart failure finally overtook him, he recovered from a serious collapse on a train to Montreal. Rushed to hospital unconscious and on the brink of death, he described afterwards the experience of calm detachment from which he observed what the doctors were doing to revive him, as if he was suspended above them in mid-air. Others who have passed through a similar experience have spoken of a vision of great light and beauty which has convinced them of the reality of life beyond death and removed from them all fear of dying.

This kind of testimony is different from the claims of spiritualists, to which I shall be referring in the next chapter. They purport to produce evidence of the continued existence of those who have actually died. I find much more impressive the testimony of those like George Gilmour who describe the experience of dying, but are reticent about anything beyond death other than a sense of light, joy and peace. In any case I do not see how experience of life in an eternal realm beyond death can be articulated in earthly terms without differentiating it from the common experience of dreaming. This was my difficulty with a recently published account of what an American woman had experienced after 'dying'.[2] She gives a detailed picture of what she claims to have discovered in the brief time before she recovered from death, and on the basis of which the course of her life was dramatically changed. I do not question her experience of dying or of a vision of what lay beyond her death. I only remain unconvinced that the details of this vision can be dissociated from dreaming or provide authentic information of an experience which lies beyond earthly comprehension.

However, for all we know, the assurance of

entering into a radically new and joyful existence may be the experience of everyone at the moment of death when physical strength slips away beyond recall. At any rate, from the standpoint of the observer the end of life may be peaceful, even if what precedes it is a struggle. The problem about dying is the way in which it is approached. The establishment and rapid development of the Hospice Movement with its use of increasingly effective painkilling drugs has transformed the treatment of the dying, and has shown the way in which dying can become a peaceful and dignified ending to life on earth.

When Dame Cecily Saunders pioneered this caring approach to the treatment of the terminally ill, she faced a good deal of suspicion and even hostility from some in the medical profession who saw it as a threat to established methods of procedure. One of the widely accepted nostrums of the professional bodies, in the social services as well as medicine, has been that emotional involvement with a client or patient should at all costs be avoided. But how can anyone be cared for as a person without the emotions being involved? The attempt to separate emotional involvement from caring can only result in treating people as things or statistics, which is the most insidious threat by the health and welfare agencies to the creation of a caring community. The challenge that the Hospice Movement in Great

Britain presents to the National Health Service underlines the criticisms which I voiced in the previous chapter, but it is a beacon of hope to those who fear the prospect of dying.

It may be of help to some who read these lines if I recount my own experience of watching my own wife's four-year battle against cancer, which ended with a triumphant five weeks in the Michael Sobel Unit attached to the Churchill Hospital in Oxford. Five years after my retirement from the presidency of the Selly Oak Colleges in Birmingham we had moved to Middleton Cheney, a little village three miles outside Banbury. I returned home one day from London to find that my wife had been to see the doctor. He had found a lump in her breast which turned out to be malignant and, in spite of a successful operation to remove it, for the next four years she fought a courageous battle against the extension of the disease, which spread to her lungs and spine and then back to her lungs. One day when we were visiting my brother in Leicestershire, Marjory found difficulty in breathing. The doctor was called and immediately sent her into hospital in Leicester where a tracheotomy was performed, leaving a pipe bypassing her throat. She returned home very frightened, not knowing how she was going to cope with what lay ahead.

Our excellent GP, Dr Large, said that he needed

to call in a specialist, and a few minutes later phoned to tell me that Dr Michael Orr would meet us at my house within the hour. What followed was a remarkable combination of medical expertise and compassionate pastoral insight. After meeting Dr Large and me in my study, he went into the living room to see Marjory. After half an hour he returned, changed the medication and said he would take on the case. Every second day for the next two weeks he came and spent half an hour with Marjory, and on the alternate days he telephoned to find out how the treatment was progressing. Such was the rapport he established with her—like Marjory he was a devout Roman Catholic and this formed a bond between them—that by the end of the fortnight he had made her angry with her condition, convinced her that God did not condemn her for this, and brought her through to complete confidence that she could face whatever lay ahead. Within a few days she developed serious lung and kidney infections, and Dr Large concluded that the best course of treatment was to have her transferred to the Hospice attached to the Churchill Hospital in Oxford.

The next five weeks were a triumphant saga of a radiant spirit mastering a rapidly weakening body. Marjory's faith was shared with fellow patients, visitors and staff alike. With the help of volunteers she sent letters and messages to all sorts of people, including all those who had played an important part in her life, and she celebrated the birthday of her small grandson by having her bed, decked with balloons, wheeled into the dayroom where the nursing staff joined in the party.

The loving care of doctors and nurses went far beyond anything that I could have anticipated. Dr Orr, whose medical treatment had been brought to a successful conclusion before Marjory was transferred to the Michael Sobel unit, unexpectedly visited her three times. On the second visit he brought a picture of the Virgin and Child for her to look at as long as she remained there, and this imaginative generosity was matched only by the sensitive and compassionate care of the nursing sisters and auxiliaries. From the moment Marjory was admitted they called her by her Christian name and established a relationship of trust which banished all fear and anxiety.

A couple of days before she died, she told me that she was in pain. I left her bed and found the young woman doctor on duty. Never shall I forget what followed. I stood at the door and watched the doctor kneel by the bed, take Marjory's hand in hers and say, 'Where is the pain, Marjory?' From that moment she began to slip peacefully away. As she did so, the sister in charge turned to me and said, 'What a beautiful death.' Indeed it was; and, more than that, it was triumphant. It may sound strange to say it, but

I believe those five weeks in the Sobel Unit were the happiest days of her life.

The funeral mass was held in Banbury and attended by a large congregation of all denominations representing the catholicity of Marjory's life and interests. Among the first to receive Communion was Dr Michael Orr, whilst our GP, Dr Large, brought up the rear of those—including Robin Woods, the former Bishop of Worcester—who came up to the altar rails to receive a blessing.

I am well aware that this experience was not a typical one. For many people, both patients and observers, it can be harrowing. But I have recounted my own wife's dying and the way in which I was privileged to participate in it to show what is possible and what actually happened within the National Health Service without any resort to private funding or exerting any special influence, though this was open for us if we had wished. This enables me to say that the experience of one grateful patient can be repeated for many others and can serve as a standard by which the care of the sick and the dying can be judged throughout the whole country.

The problems of the National Health Service, as I have said, are not primarily due to the lack of money, but to the way in which finance is administered and used. Where policy is dominated by statistics and not by the quality of care, patients are bound to suffer and the prospect of dying will be regarded with fear and foreboding.

This has direct bearing on the controversial question of euthanasia. The reasons advanced against legalizing this practice are generally based on the sacredness of life and the doctor's Hippocratic oath to preserve life as far as is medically possible. To these are added tortuous legal arguments about the impossibility of ensuring that it would not be abused by relatives taking advantage of those who are weak and whose faculties have become impaired. It is not altogether surprising that many people are unconvinced by these arguments when they take into account the suffering of the terminally ill.

The achievements of the Hospice Movement provide a far more powerful argument against euthanasia than those usually advanced. They point to the positive value of overcoming suffering and enhancing the quality of life of those who are terminally ill. My wife battled against the ravages of cancer for over four years, but she would not have foregone the enrichment of her experience and the fulfilment of her life in those final five weeks; nor would I have wished her to do so. Admittedly, her own attitude and the faith which sustained her enabled her to use that time as constructively as she did, and she probably contributed as much to the doctors, nurses and caring friends as they did to her. To die positively with hope is of much more value than to live any number of years.

While I believe this kind of experience is a decisive argument against euthanasia as generally advocated, there remains the problem of keeping patients artificially alive when they have lost consciousness and are beyond the power of medical treatment to revive them. Advances in techniques have made this increasingly practicable in recent years. Through the invention of antibiotics the days of the natural death of old people from pneumonia are over. There is an overwhelming case against the merely artificial prolongation of life, and the practice is growing of drawing up, as I have done, what are called 'living wills' to make that clear. Where no such wills have been made, a decision to shut off a life-support machine or stop administering medication should be left to the discretion of the doctors in consultation with the relatives. This is not euthanasia, understood as positive steps taken to terminate life, but the refusal to prolong it artificially.

Of course, all that I have said about Marjory's battle against cancer and triumphant death took place against the background of her faith and that of those who cared for her. The doctors and sisters in the Sobel Unit shared with her the belief that life on earth was only a prelude to what lay ahead. This made all the difference to the serenity with which she approached the end of her journey, confident in the Christian hope and assured of the support and companionship of the risen Christ in the midst of suffering.

However, the same peaceful ending to life is also available to the unbeliever, even if he or she has no hope for the future and no awareness of the divine resources which are at hand. When we are helpless at the end of life, we are entirely dependent on the caring of others, and that is something which we cannot control or deserve. Faith in God makes all the difference to the way in which we approach dying, but it does not affect the availability of the *resources* to us, whoever we are, as we come to the end of our days on earth. Therefore, this chapter is applicable to everyone, believer and unbeliever alike. Without faith or hope, love still remains, according to Paul's great trilogy,[3] though for the atheist it does not endure. The threefold promise alone gives us ultimate assurance of the meaningful fulfilment of life.

Chapter Eight

Life After Death

Is there a life beyond death and, if so, what is it like?
Is it like anything on earth and, if not, how can we
possibly conceive it? Answering these questions raises
a host of problems and, even if we have reason to
hope that death is not the extinction of human
personality, we may find that we have no categories
of thought or imagination to say anything convincing
about the future which awaits us.

In past ages there was widespread belief in a
world beyond this one in which human beings would
fulfil their ultimate destiny. Was that the product of
wishful thinking or was it grounded in experience
available to us while still on earth? Many would argue
that the belief is nothing but superstition and that
the very idea is a logical impossibility resting on the
assumption that the mind or soul can be separated
from the body. We know that the latter perishes,
returning to dust and ashes. What sense then can be
made of the claim that anything can survive the
dissolution of the flesh?

The cavalier dismissal of the possibility of anything surviving death rests on the assumption that human beings can be defined exclusively in bodily terms. This was denied by Plato as long ago as the fifth century before Christ when, in his famous dialogues, he maintained that the soul is immortal, imprisoned within the body until released by death. Such dualism has been taken for granted in many different cultures, as is evidenced by the elaborate burial practices in ancient Egypt and elsewhere. Those in modern times who have contended for the continuity of the body as the sole criterion of personal identity have had to face the fact that the physical organism changes and decays throughout a lifetime while the self-conscious person persists and develops. Memory, rather than observable bodily elements, guarantees the persistence of a human being through time. As Professor A.E. Taylor, the eminent Scottish philosopher, says in his book on the subject, 'We are never safe in declaring that anything which our senses cannot detect must be nothing at all.'[1]

Nevertheless, there has been a growing consensus that, even if purely physicalist accounts of the human personality prove to be unable to cover all the data of experience, persons have to be defined in unitary terms as psycho-physical organisms of which the body is a necessary component. Questions then arise about the possibility of personal existence beyond death without the body. This is the problem which thorough-going dualists who follow Plato in believing in the immortality of the soul have to face. Christians counter that by affirming the unity of the person and the need for a means of expression for the personality beyond death. Therefore, the Christian doctrine of the after-life is of the resurrection of the body, not the immortality of the soul, as essential to a full personal life in the eternal realm.

The resurrection of the body does not mean the resuscitation of the flesh, but the provision of a new instrument, adapted to the life beyond just as the physical body is adapted to life on earth. This carries with it the conviction that there is nothing which automatically survives death. We really do die and, left to ourselves, that would be the end of everything as far as we are concerned. But the Christian faith is that the life beyond is a new creation by God for which a new 'body' is provided which allows for the intercommunication of persons without which any concept of life beyond death would be devoid of value. To quote Professor A.E. Taylor again:

The Christian's 'world to come' is not one of solitary speculation, but one where the members love one another, are united in the 'bond of charity'; and such a relation between persons who are irreducibly separate—for if they were not, they could not love one another—demands a 'body' in the sense of a medium of intercommunication of thought and affection. But, as the Apostle was careful to say, that body is a 'spiritual' one; we 'shall all be changed', and none of us knows what that change may involve... how this may be effected, we have no more than the information 'God giveth it a body as it hath pleased Him'.²

This distinction between the Christian doctrine of the resurrection of the body and the Greek concept of the immortality of the soul meets, I believe, the objections to dualism, and safeguards the unity of personality which is inherent in our understanding of human beings as essentially psychosomatic. The Christian doctrine does not leave us with the idea of the survival of disembodied ghosts or the mere continuation of the kind of life we live here on earth. That would be the most dreary prospect: an endless succession of trivialities. Christianity holds out the hope that eternal life is infinitely richer than life on earth. Although we cannot imagine its content, we are given the assurance that 'What no eye has seen, nor ear heard, nor the heart of man conceived, what God has prepared for those who love him, God has revealed to us through the Spirit.'³

In the *Phaedo* Plato asked the rhetorical question: 'Shall we believe that the soul, whose nature is so glorious and pure and invisible, is blown away by the winds, and perishes as soon as she leaves the body as the world says?'[4] In spite of the appeal this has made and continues to make to many people—for it strikes the chord that what is of ultimate value cannot perish—the idea of mere survival, if that is what it means, falls far short of the promise that eternal life beyond the grave exceeds anything that we have experienced on earth. Moreover, it implies that there is inherent in us that which has the capacity of itself to survive death: an assumption which becomes more and more questionable as we come to realize our mortal weakness—a basic defect of which the saints have been acutely aware. The doctrine of the resurrection puts the emphasis on the *creative action of God*, not on the inherent capacity of human beings for survival.

While this affords a tenable account of the possibility of life after death, it does not of itself provide grounds for a convincing argument that such a destiny does in fact await us. There are those who claim that we have evidence from actual experiences while still on earth. In the previous chapter I referred to the testimony of some of those who have been on the brink of death or even claim to have been beyond it and yet regained their physical faculties. I find these experiences far more convincing than those adduced by the advocates of spiritualism, whose evidence still seems to be open to dubious interpretation and often reflects merely trivial information about the after-life.[5] A more serious objection to relying on such evidence was advanced by William Temple, the wartime Archbishop of Canterbury, who maintained that it detracted from our dependence on the creative acts and promises of God:

As far as I can see, it is positively undesirable that there should be experimental proof of man's survival of death... it would certainly, as I think, make very much harder the essential business of faith, which is the transference of the centre of interest from the self to God. If such knowledge comes, it must be accepted, and we must try to use it for good and not for evil.[6]

Temple's conviction about the reality of life after death rested on other grounds. In a letter to his wife he wrote: 'There is nothing in the world of which I feel so certain: I have no idea what it will be like and I think I am glad that I have not, as I am sure it would be wrong.'[7] What made him so sure? Like Benjamin Jowett, the famous Master of Balliol College, his belief in life after death was based on his belief in God. In writing about Plato, Jowett said:

If God exists, then the soul exists after death; and if there is no God, there is no existence of the soul after death. We are more certain of the existence of God than we are of the immortality of the soul, and are led by the belief in the one to the belief in the other.[8]

Temple based his certainty on the same conviction:

*If God is righteous—still more if God is love—
immortality follows as a consequence. He made me; He
loves me; He will not let me perish, so long as there is
anything in me that he can love.*[9]

This is firmer ground than basing belief on the
conviction that the moral incompleteness of life here
on earth demands an eternal world in which the
imperfections of this one will be redressed: 'Heaven
shall make perfect our imperfect life.' Following Kant,
that has carried conviction for many others, such as
Professor Taylor who developed it at length in his
famous Gifford Lectures, 'The Faith of a Moralist'.[10]

While this is a persuasive line of argument from
the philosophical point of view—and I would not wish
to discount it—it carries with it the danger, if pressed
too far and if too much reliance is placed upon it, of
putting the emphasis in the wrong place: on human
aspirations and achievements rather than on the
everlasting mercy of God. Both Temple and Taylor
would agree that the moral argument is sustained by
belief in the creative initiative of God which is
guaranteed by the resurrection of Jesus Christ from
the dead and by his promise, 'Because I live, you will
live also'.[11] Paul underlined and spelt this out in his
chapter on the implications of the resurrection of

Jesus in his first letter to the Corinthians.[12]

In an earlier chapter I referred to General Sir John Shea who, as Scout Commissioner for London, was such a source of encouragement during the dark days of the Luftwaffe's blitz on Dockland. One day he asked me if I could lend him a book on life after death. I found one on my shelves which he returned some weeks later with the quaint but impressive comment, 'I found the book interesting, but I prefer to trust the word of a gentleman.' This was his way of saying that the words of Jesus, 'In my father's house are many mansions; if it were not so I would have told you',[13] were good enough for him.

However, questions remain for those who accept the Christian doctrine of the resurrection. What kind of existence awaits us as eternal life beyond the grave? Do we enter into it immediately at the point of death or do we sleep, awaiting the general resurrection at the end of time? Will we be reunited with our families and friends? Do differing destinies await us—heaven or hell—and, if so, what will be the basis of discrimination and judgment? We may have to confess that we are in no position to answer any of these questions and must rest on confidence in the goodness and mercy of God. But the questions are real ones and they will not go away. At least we should try to discover how far answers are available to us and recognize the limits of our understanding.

The question about heaven and hell is the most pressing and perplexing one. There are those who dismiss the idea of hell altogether, whether conceived as the destiny of unbelievers or of those judged morally guilty, on the ground that a loving God would not reject any of his creatures or allow his purpose for creation to be frustrated and fail. On the other hand, universalism of this kind seems to make nonsense of human freedom and moral responsibility and, it is held, both the Bible and the Christian tradition make the distinction, whether the destiny of the rebellious and damned is conceived as extinction, penalization or self-inflicted abandonment. This belief that hell or extinction awaits vast numbers is strengthened by the reality of hell on earth when God's promises are ignored or abandoned and selfishness, hatred, cruelty and moral degeneracy are allowed to prevail.

I do not pretend to know the final answers to the questions these alternatives raise. Their resolution lies in the hands of God, but I believe some clue is granted us from reflection on the good news of the life, death and resurrection of Jesus. If the redemption of creation, including the human race, was achieved by God through him, and if he alone is the guarantor of eternal life beyond death, then to assume that moral achievement or even faith can earn this reward is a fundamental mistake. I confess that I have been greatly influenced in holding to this conclusion by the writings of the great Swiss theologian, Karl Barth,[14] even if I cannot begin to see how God works it out in the end. Barth maintains that the redemption which Christ Jesus wrought was for all, available to all, whether they recognize it or not.

This means that if hell on earth is perpetuated in the life beyond because of alienation from God through the free choice of men and women, the way back in repentance is always open and the glories of heaven available to anyone who awakens to their true heritage. The love of God remains unalterably the same for those in heaven and hell. The difference between them is that those in heaven have come to realize it and glory in it while those in hell have not. C.S. Lewis portrayed this brilliantly in allegorical form when he described hell as a dismal city where only a few took up the offer of a bus ride to heaven, while the rest lived a dreary existence in alienation from their neighbours.[15] Reconciliation with God and our neighbours is inseparable. Heaven is when both have become a reality; hell is when both have been abandoned. But eternity is the realm where both are on offer as a free and unmerited gift.

This is why I cannot accept the dogmatism of those who claim that the destiny of human beings is finally settled either by their moral behaviour or by their faith on earth. To make such a claim seems to me to rely on our human frailty rather than on the infinite power of God to transform creation through what our ancestors called 'the finished work of Christ'. I shall return to this theme in the final chapter when I ask what realistic hope we can have for the future of the human race within the context of God's creation. Here I leave the question of the ultimate destiny of the individual still clouded in mystery: mystery which cannot be resolved on earth, but ultimately is in the hands of One whose face has been seen in Jesus Christ.

This seems to me to provide the assurance for which many people look when they lose relatives or friends and wonder whether they will ever meet them again. In reflecting on the values which endure I maintained that it was human relationships which turned out to be of ultimate importance, and these cannot therefore be broken by death:

Death hides, but it does not divide -
Thou art but on Christ's other side;
Thou art with Christ and Christ with me.
In him I still am close to thee.[16]

We do not have to assume that these relationships will simply continue to bind us to one another in the same way as they did on earth; they will be raised to a higher and deeper level than anything we have known in this life. Surely that is what Jesus meant when replying to the trick question put to him by the Sadducees. They asked him whose wife a woman would be who had seven brothers as husbands in turn, following the practice of the brother of a dead man taking his widow as his wife. In replying that when people rise from the dead, they 'neither marry nor are given in marriage, but are like angels in heaven',[17] he was not denying the continuance of a loving relationship, but rather declaring that it was lifted on to a higher plane.

On earth our relationships are limited, but in heaven they may be infinitely enlarged. In one of her famous novels George Eliot perceptively wrote:

If we had a keen vision and feeling of all ordinary human life, it would be like hearing the grass grow and the squirrel's heart beat, and we should die of that roar which lies on the other side of silence. As it is, the quickest of us walk about well wadded with stupidity.[18]

That is inevitable under earthly conditions. However wide our circle of relatives and friends, our capacity for personal relationships is limited. The idea of its infinite extension in the life beyond helps us to resolve what is otherwise the intractable problem of the significance of the individual in a mass society. The doctrine of the Communion of Saints enshrined in the Christian creeds offers the promise of entering into close relationship not only with those we have known on earth, but with those of past ages and ages to come. Our imaginations may not be equal to this when we are confined to an existence in space and time, but there is no reason why we should not hope that 'upon another shore and in a greater light' with them 'we are for ever one'.[19]

Is this an experience we can anticipate when we die or does it have to await the end of time? I suspect that this only appears to be an alternative since we are conditioned on earth to think in terms of the passage of chronological time, whereas eternity is the ever present 'Now'. This would mean that from the standpoint of eternity our death would coincide with the death of this temporal and spatial universe. Therefore, I see no reason why we should not think of, pray for and be in unseen communion with those whom we have loved on earth and lost for a little while, and believe that all our temporal deaths are taken up into the consummation of all things in eternity.

As I look back on what I have written in this chapter, I am conscious of how little I know and how limited is my imagination. But as I approach the imminent adventure of death I pray that, to use a phrase coined by one of our most eminent historians, I may be enabled to 'hold on to Christ, and for the rest be totally uncommitted'.[20]

Chapter Nine

Hope for the Future

What prospect is there for the future of the human race and life on this planet? Has the universe as we know it an indefinite future or will it end in oblivion? We cannot possibly know the answer to the second of these questions although, as my former college principal used to say, it seems logical to assume that what had a beginning must have an end. However, it is the first of these questions that concerns us because, as with the limited scope of our relationships on earth to which I referred in the last chapter, the question becomes purely theoretical beyond the time of our grandchildren or perhaps great-grandchildren. We may talk in abstract terms about future generations, but our real concern is limited to those who are in some way directly related to us.

If this seems to limit our questioning unduly, I

find it curious that speculation about the ultimate future of life on earth seems to occupy so much attention in both religious and secular circles when the end of the world for each of us is so certainly imminent in our own deaths. That is why I think that the questions raised in the last chapter are more important than the more general question about the prospect for the human race; for however many generations of human beings may yet be born, they will still have to face the same imminent end to their lives as we do. That is, of course, unless one of the nightmares of science fiction were to come to pass, the indefinite prolongation of life on earth—a prospect too awful to contemplate!

However, we are rightly concerned about the future of our grandchildren and their descendents, and we want to be assured that they face a better prospect than we have done. In exploring this we shall, I believe, find further illumination on the future that awaits us all on the other side of death.

The secular prospect today offers little ground for hope. The expansion of knowledge and the advancement of science and technology in the nineteenth century encouraged the idea that the human race was on the threshold of a period of indefinite progress. Optimism was the order of the day. But the twentieth century has seen these hopes dashed to the ground by the slaughter of two world wars and the spread of national, ethnic and racial conflicts, as well as by the common acceptance that cruelty and violence on a wide scale is a natural and intractable phenomenon of the modern world. The spectacular advances we have seen in science and technology may have brought great benefits in medicine, communication and industrial productivity—although these have been accompanied by unforeseen problems, such as the devotion of resources to quantifiable growth at the expense of human welfare and the preservation of the environment. But these advances have also put into human hands sophisticated means of destruction and exploitation which would have been unimaginable in previous generations.

In addition to the growing problem of the pollution of the environment and the wanton misuse and depletion of the earth's natural resources, the threat of a nuclear holocaust has hung over the world like a storm cloud on the horizon, foreshadowing destruction on such a scale as to jeopardize the continuance of life on this planet. In a book published at the height of the cold war, the director of research into aviation technology at Farnborough calculated that the balance of probability was weighted against the human race surviving beyond the end of the twentieth century.[1] This gloomy forecast receded into the background as the world breathed a sigh of relief at the collapse of Marxist communism and the end of the cold war.

But the euphoria began to dissipate as people came to realize that this had opened the way to the outbreak of more limited national, tribal and racial conflicts, with the threat of irresponsible terrorism as a growing menace.

We may have made spectacular scientific and technological advances in the twentieth century, but human nature has remained the same. We may have become more clever, but instead of this making us better able to handle the problems confronting us, it seems to have increased our powers of cruelty and destruction. Yet alongside these we have massive evidence of human kindness, compassion and generosity, both in neighbourly relationships and in charitable munificence in response to all kinds of appeals for good causes. We are a strange mixture of good and evil, and we are caught in structures not of our individual devising, but within which we are powerless to effect any change for the better except at rare intervals when we can exercise our franchise or when we are motivated to join pressure groups, the influence of which is generally severely limited. Apart from the personal calamities which may befall us, the greed and lust for power which are built into the framework of society threaten not only our own welfare, but that of our families, friends and neighbours, not to speak of any generations that may succeed us. In the light of this, what hope can we have for the immediate future, let alone the next millennium? Faced with these questions it is not surprising that most people shrug their shoulders and hope we can muddle through.

This is the best that a sober view of history and a realistic appraisal of the state of modern society have to offer: the promises of improving the human situation are liable to be swamped by the destructive forces in which we appear to be engulfed. That is why from a secular point of view this may be characterized as the hopeless generation. But has secularism the last word? Does religion, and Christianity in particular, provide grounds for hope that, in spite of all appearances, the purpose of God for his creation will ultimately come to fruition?

There are various answers to this question. Some Christians still share with optimistic humanists the belief that common sense and goodwill must ultimately prevail. This was a popular view, particularly among Americans, in the earlier part of the twentieth century and is still pretty widely held. In this view the good news proclaimed by Jesus was the establishment of the kingdom of God on earth, the reign of righteousness, justice and peace which he had inaugurated and which he called his followers to promote. This closely accords with popular conceptions of what should be the business of the Church, even though many politicians would like to restrict it to the sphere of what they suppose to be private morals.

This outlook now appears not only dated, but wholly unrealistic in the light of the dominance of evil in the modern world, at the root of which is sin. This is properly understood as rebellion against and alienation from God, not simply as the breaking of a moral code. It cannot be said too forcibly and clearly that the identification of religion with morals is a superficial analysis of the human situation; moral standards are grounded in a right relationship with God which is dependent on penitence and trust, and moral exhortation falls on deaf ears when men and women are bent on pursuing their own selfish interests. In the light of the news which appears in our daily papers and on our television screens it is sheer obscurantism to place our hope for the future in the ability of human beings to shape the destiny of the race and safeguard the welfare of generations yet to come.

An alternative approach is to give up this world for lost and pin all our hopes on the dramatic intervention of God to bring history to a close and establish his universal reign. This takes many forms associated with the return of Christ to earth, often based on literal and dubious interpretations of the imagery of the Bible. No clear and convincing picture emerges from these speculations, and many Christians would be hard put to it to say whether they look to the return of Christ to reign on earth, as millenarians have maintained, or to the end of history and the establishment of the kingdom of God in the eternal world when this one is no more. The promise of a 'new heaven and a new earth'[2] can be interpreted either way. But, whatever the expectation, it entails abandonment of this world and setting aside the Lord's prayer that his kingdom should come and his will be done on earth as it is done in heaven. In any case, as I have already argued, the end of this world for all of us comes inevitably after a short span of years. That undeniable fact has to be integrated with the apocalyptic expectations of those who look to the end of the present world by its transformation here—in which event the resurrection of the dead would be to a transformed life on earth—or to their resurrection to life in an eternal world which is beyond the death of everyone. This approach to the question of the future of the human race usually carries with it the belief that salvation is a purely individual matter and is restricted to those who have put their faith in Christ while here on earth. All others are lost or condemned to hell, however that may be conceived.

This interpretation of the Bible and Christian

tradition seems to me to be open to several serious objections. In the first place, it is narrowly exclusivist, denying all hope to those who lived before Christ or who have never heard the gospel, to the adherents of all the other great religious traditions and to all those who for one reason or another have never committed themselves to orthodox Christian faith. Such an exclusivist dogma seems hard, if not impossible, to reconcile with belief in the God of justice and mercy as revealed by the Lord Jesus Christ.

Secondly, it places far too much weight on the constancy of a person's faith. Those who are honest with themselves know how frail is their hold on the promise of eternal life and how dependent they are on the grace of God. I have often found myself quoting words from an unknown source:

Let me no more my comfort draw
From my frail hold on Thee;
In this alone rejoice with awe -
Thy mighty grasp on me.

One of the main emphases of this book has been reliance on the creative activity of God as the only guarantee of eternal life. Those who interpret the teaching of the Bible in exclusivist terms do not seem to realize the danger of turning faith into a human achievement and thereby claiming that salvation can be earned. Faith is an *awakening* to the awareness of our heritage in Christ, not the means to *achieving* it.

Thirdly, the interpretation which I have been criticizing is mistakenly individualistic. It does not take into account the fact that we are bound up with others in the bundle of life and that we are what we are in relationship to other people. 'Where are the others?' God will ask us if we presume to go to him alone. This is of particular importance to Christians who have lost loved ones about whose faith they may have serious doubts or who, they recognize, had no faith at all. Are they irretrievably lost? If so, what are we to make of the ties that bind us not only to those in our intimate circle of love and friendship, but to the rest of the human family? If, as I have contended, ultimate value lies in human relationships and these are what endure and are preserved to all eternity, thorough-going individualism seems to be precluded in the providence of God. The parables of the lost coin, the lost sheep and the lost son in the fifteenth chapter of Luke's Gospel simply underline the question, 'Where are the others?'

Finally—and this brings us to the heart of the matter—those who give up the world for lost are implicitly denying the doctrine of the incarnation— that in the coming of Jesus God took upon himself human nature and wrought its redemption through his death on the cross and the triumph of his resurrection. God did not escape or reject the world he had created, but immersed himself in it. He took upon himself the burden of our sin, all our cruelty, pride, selfishness and maliciousness, and made eternal life available to us all. The *cosmos* was redeemed, not just the human race and certainly not a select few individuals. The escapist answer to the question of human destiny makes nonsense of our actual involvement with the affairs of this world and their redemption which is the heart of the Christian faith.

What then do I believe the future holds and what, how and when will be the end of the human story on earth? I do not know. That, as Jesus said,[3] is in the hands of God. But I believe the apocalypse, or unveiling of the eternal world, will be no different for the last survivors on earth than for the rest of us at the moment of death. John's Gospel records Jesus as saying:

Let not your hearts be troubled; believe in God, believe also in me. In my Father's house are many rooms; if it were not so, would I have told you that I go and prepare a place for you? And when I go and prepare a place for you, I will come again and will take you to myself, that where I am you may be also.[4]

That is enough for me as I face my own death and contemplate the end of human life on earth whenever that may be.

This entails taking an entirely different view of history from that which is commonly taught in schools and universities. The decisive events in history are not the rise and fall of empires or the wars which have ravaged nations and continents. Nor is there any ultimate significance in the achievements of human beings in politics, architecture, art, music or scientific discovery except in so far as they contribute to the development of human character and relationships. 'If', as a former Cambridge historian writes,' the end of history lies in personalities, which represent the highest things we know in the mundane realm, then we must face the fact that the purpose of history is not something that lies a thousand years ahead of us—it is constantly here, always with us, for ever achieving itself—the end of human history is the manufacture and education of human souls.'[5] If that is so, the centre of history and its decisive point was the coming of Jesus Christ, the kingdom he inaugurated and the transformation of the cosmos and the human condition which he accomplished through his death and resurrection. Everything which contributes to the establishment of peace and justice or the development of creative relationships under the sovereignty of God has enduring value. Nothing else matters.

This enables us to regard the evil of the world as ultimately overcome. We do not need to expect that it will disappear in some future utopia. The kingdoms of this world will continue to flourish or disintegrate to the end of time, but they will be overlapped and finally superseded by the kingdom of God. Instead of the Christian community being marginalized and driven to the fringes of society, it can be seen to be at its very heart, widely unrecognized, but witnessing to and promoting that which has enduring value. This means taking whatever steps lie within our power here and now to strengthen that witness and work for the advancement of the kingdom of God for which Jesus taught us to pray.

It is difficult to keep this in view when faced with rampant and organized evil as we have so often been in the last hundred years. In the midst of the Second World War, Dr Van Dusen, the President of Union Theological Seminary in New York, wrote:

When we pause to think, we know that the blackout is never wholly complete. Only to the external view does it appear so. Behind the blinds which convey to the outside world a semblance of utter darkness, lights are still burning—shaded, guarded, kept perhaps secretly aflame, sometimes only tiny flickers. So it is with the world's life in this hour. To the external eye, to the superficial view, almost total blackout. To keener discernment, behind the darkness lights still burn— sometimes mere flickers, sometimes gravely menaced, sometimes only secretly, sometimes with fierce though hidden flame. From those candles and lamps, scattered across the face of this war-stricken and war-darkened world, shall come the flames which shall yet rekindle the lights of humanity—flames kept alight from Him who is the light of the world. They shall give their illumination until that day comes in when 'there shall be no night nor need of a candle, nor light of the sun; for the Lord shall give light'. Our task, yours and mine, is to keep those lights burning.[6]

That was no utopian vision of the coming of the kingdom of God on earth, but a summons to keep the lights of the kingdom burning whatever the encompassing darkness; for, to use the words of the Prologue to the Fourth Gospel, 'The light shines in the darkness, and the darkness has not overcome it.'[7] That is the Christian hope.

Notes to chapters

CHAPTER ONE: GROWING OLDER

1 Rudyard Kipling, 'The Return'.

2 *Leading Light*, Vol. 2/1, Winter 1995.

3 Hannah Whittall Smith, *A Religious Rebel*, ed. Logan Pearsall Smith, Nisbet, 1949.

4 Whittall Smith, *A Religious Rebel*, pp. 156f.

5 *An Ecumenical Pilgrimage*, West Ham Central Mission, 1994.

CHAPTER TWO: THE STOREHOUSE OF MEMORY

1 Thomas Hood (1799-1845), 'I Remember' (1826).

CHAPTER FOUR: REFLECTIONS ON EXPERIENCE

1 Ecclesiasticus 25:4-6 (NEB).

2 E.L. Mascall, *Saraband*, Gracewing, 1995, pp. 191f.

3 Luke 9:25.

4 Luke 12:20.

5 Matthew 26:52.

6 Herbert Butterfield, *Christianity and History*, Bell, 1949, p. 104

CHAPTER FIVE: THE PROBLEM OF LONELINESS

1 Elizabeth Templeton, 'The Church's Task in Reconciliation', *Theology*, Vol. XCIV, September/October 1991, pp. 326-32.

2 Matthew 5:44-45 (NEB).

3 John 6:37 (NEB).

CHAPTER SIX: FACING INFIRMITY

1 C.S. Lewis, *The Problem of Pain*, Bles, 1940.

2 Psalm 46:1.

3 John 9:2.

4 Job 42:2-6 (NEB).

5 John 9:3

6 Hebrews 2:18 (NEB).

7 W.E. Henley, 'Invictus'.

CHAPTER SEVEN: THE ADVENTURE OF DYING

1 Francis Bacon, *Essays*, 2. 'Of Death'.

2 Betty Eadie, *Embraced by the Light*, HarperCollins, 1993.

3 1 Corinthians 13:13.

CHAPTER EIGHT: LIFE AFTER DEATH

1 A. E. Taylor, *The Christian Hope of Immortality*, Centenary Press, 1939, p. 17.

2 Taylor, *The Christian Hope of Immortality*, pp. 74f.

3 1 Corinthians 2:9. Cf. Isaiah 64:4 and 65:17.

4 Plato, *Phaedo* 7.9.

5 Cf. Taylor, *The Christian Hope of Immortality*, pp. 19-21.

6 William Temple, *Nature, Man and God*, Macmillan, 1934.

7 F. A. Iremonger, *William Temple*, Oxford University Press, 1963, p. 626.

8 Benjamin Jowett, *On Plato*, Princetown, 1996 (distributed by Oxford University Press).

9 Temple, *Nature, Man and God*, p. 457.

10 A. E. Taylor, *The Faith of a Moralist*, Macmillan, 1931, Series I, pp. 67ff.

11 John 14:19.

12 1 Corinthians 15, especially verses 16-19.

13 John 14:2 (AV).

14 Karl Barth, *Church Dogmatics*, T. & T. Clark, 1980, IV.3.2., pp. 795ff. and throughout.

15 C.S. Lewis, *The Great Divorce*, Bles, 1945.

16 Patterson Smythe, *The Gospel of the Hereafter*.

17 Mark 12:25.

18 George Eliot, *Middlemarch*, The Warwick Edition, Blackwood, 1892, Vol. I, p. 297f.

19 Preface to the Carol Service at King's College, Cambridge.

20 Herbert Butterfield, *Christianity and History*, Bell, 1949, p. 146.

CHAPTER NINE: HOPE FOR THE FUTURE

1 Desmond King-Hele, *The End of the Twentieth Century*, Macmillan, 1970.

2 Revelation 21:1.

3 Mark 13:32.

4 John 14:1-3.

5 Butterfield, *Christianity and History*, Bell, 1949, p. 76.

6 P. Van Dusen, *What is the Church Doing?*, SCM, 1943, pp. 116-17.

7 John 1:5.